BUILDING SCIENCE 101

A Primer for Librarians

Lynn M. Piotrowicz and Scott Osgood

AMERICAN LIBRARY ASSOCIATION
CHICAGO 2010

Lynn M. Piotrowicz has been a librarian in old buildings for seventeen years. As the director of a 105-year-old building, she sought information to bring utility costs under control and reduce her library's dependence on nonrenewable resources. Piotrowicz has a BA in psychology (Mercyhurst College, 1986), an MA in organizational psychology (University of New Haven, 1988), and an MLS (University of Pittsburgh, 1992). She is director of the Tucker Free Library in Henniker, New Hampshire. Scott Osgood is a registered professional civil engineer with more than thirty years' experience in the building construction industry. He is the director of facilities and capital projects for the seven-campus Community College System of New Hampshire, with responsibility for the construction, renovation, and care of more than fifty buildings. Osgood has a BS in civil engineering from the University of Massachusetts.

The paper used in this publication meets the minimum requirements of American National Standard for Information Sciences—Permanence of Paper for Printed Library Materials, ANSI Z39.48-1992. ♾

Library of Congress Cataloging-in-Publication Data
Piotrowicz, Lynn M.
    Building science 101 : a primer for librarians / Lynn M. Piotrowicz and Scott Osgood.
        p. cm.
    Includes index.
    ISBN 978-0-8389-1041-2 (alk. paper)
    1. Library buildings—Remodeling—United States. 2. Library buildings—Conservation and restoration—United States. 3. Library buildings—Energy conservation—United States. 4. Library buildings—Design and construction—United States. I. Osgood, Scott. II. Title.
Z679.2.U54P56 2010
022'.31--dc22

                                                                            2009047677

ISBN-13: 978-0-8389-1041-2

Printed in the United States of America
14 13 12 11 10   5 4 3 2 1

This book is dedicated to my muse, my friend, my partner, and my excuse not to work on Sundays, Terri Rounds, and to our great cocker spaniel, Thomas, who really did eat my paper! To DSO for always coming to my aid at TFL when PO suggests an engineer look at our projects and for always giving the best advice!

Also, to the trustees and staff of the Tucker Free Library for all the support and reassurances provided during my years there!
—LMP

I dedicate this book to my girls (Patti included) and to LMP, because you really care about buildings, and getting it right.
—SO

CONTENTS

INTRODUCTION

A **S YOU ENTER** your building on a snowy morning, do you marvel at the beautiful icicles that drip down from the roof? As you look out your office window, do you express childish glee over the work of Jack Frost on your panes? Does your staff suddenly look thinner in April because they've started removing the multiple layers of their winter wardrobe? Does your library offer the same summer reading program every year, "Reading in the Tropics," because then shorts, T-shirts, and sandals are the approved "uniform" for your staff, which is working in a building that feels like the rain forest: hazy, hot, and humid?

Although many librarians accept responsibility for their town libraries, a good number of us do so based on the merits of our experience providing excellent library service. This includes our outstanding collection development philosophy, our creative ability, and our extraordinary multitasking skills that allow us simultaneously to develop programs, complete our own cataloging, build a web page, maintain a blog, and conduct business at the reference desk. Many of us proudly wear the badge of a liberal arts or humanities major with very little science background. Some of us took our obligatory science class during the first semester of our freshman year and haven't given much, if any, thought to the difference between an atom and a molecule since. Few of us have any experience managing our library's physical plant: the structure of the facility, the bones of our building. Sure, we may have helped shovel snow, put up storm windows, or open vents, but those acts do not constitute knowledge of a building. Specifically, we often have very little experience with thermal heat gain, the stack effect, kilowatts, conduction or convection, HVAC, Energy Star ratings, the R-value, or U-factors.

The first year I managed my library, No. 2 heating oil jumped from 89 cents per gallon to $1.69 per gallon; the next year it increased to $2.49 per gallon, then $2.69 per gallon, and then our prepaid contract skyrocketed to $4.59 per gallon. During those first three years I had been looking for ways to reduce the cost of utilities at our library, but during the 2008–2009 heating season it became obvious that we still needed to do more. We had already installed programmable thermostats and set them, much to my staff's chagrin, at 67°, only to see our utility bills continue to rise.

I recently attended a session at a regional conference that seemed like it would answer my question: "What can we do to make our town library more energy efficient?" The room was filled with over fifty library directors. Before the presentation started the audience members were asked to introduce themselves and then talk briefly about their buildings (age, materials used, etc.). Most audience members were directors of library buildings over fifty years old, with many well over seventy-five years old, and a few buildings were one hundred or more years old (including my own). There was excitement in the room! We were going to learn something about reducing the operating expense of our buildings that we could take back to our communities!

My enthusiasm quickly waned as it became apparent that the presenters were going to provide case studies of their brand-new, LEED-certified, state-of-the-art buildings. As the presentation progressed, I listened to some of the questions that members of the audience were asking. It became obvious that there were many librarians who were trying to make a difference, but who didn't see a building program that involved the replacement of their town jewel as an option! When asked, the presenters were unable to answer the basic question: "But what are some simple things that we can do to make our humble buildings more energy efficient?" As I was driving home, I came to the conclusion that answering this question would become my professional quest. In my research I found there was no one place I could turn to for the answer, so I thought I would answer the question myself and share it with all those audience members (and with the readers of this book). I contacted my favorite local engineer, and he agreed that this book needed to be written and he would be my coauthor.

If you are managing the "ole town library," you have the unique honor and challenge of being a steward of a long-standing institution in your community.

With this comes many obstacles, but it also gives you the opportunity to learn about the beautiful intricacies of an architecturally unique resource. You have the chance to make a significant impact on the preservation of a local treasure, as well as creating a comfortable space within it.

Why is this book important? Because a quick survey of program descriptions and course lists for ALA-accredited library school programs shows that few offer any formal classes in the area of *building maintenance* or *facilities management*. Many of us are learning about our buildings on the job. We learn about power surges or mold or other physical aspects of our buildings when we are in the midst of a crisis, which is the worst time to deal with new information. Just as it is crucial to have a solid disaster plan in place (and if you don't, you need to read another book when you finish this one), it is essential to look at your physical plant before something goes wrong—and this book will help you do just that.

With utility costs continuing to fluctuate wildly, an older library building will cost you more money, becoming a liability because it is draining your budget to cover simple operational expenses such as heating and cooling. The fact remains that the library needs to be open and comfortable for your patrons. But if more of your money is being channeled into heating and cooling, then there is less money available for acquisitions, programs, personnel, and technology. This book will show you how to look at your building with a critical eye. It will instruct you on what data you should be collecting for the long-term cost-benefit analysis of your proposed improvements. It will help you understand the physical dynamics of your building so you can manage it better. It will help you keep your building in a state of excellent repair, and that will help decrease the energy consumed by the building.

This book is titled *Building Science 101: A Primer for Librarians* because it gives you some of the basic tools you will need. It will prepare you to examine the efficiency of your building, talk to the professionals who can help you with your various projects, and give you the confidence and credibility you need to seek funding for those projects. If you know the names and functions of various building components, then it is much easier for you to justify why projects such as adding insulation, weatherproofing windows, adding energy-efficient window treatments, and light retrofitting need to be done. If you understand how the major systems such as heating, cooling, or your roof work, then when they need replacing you will be a more articulate advocate for alternative systems. This book will provide library decision makers with the vocabulary and knowledge to create a systematic, incremental plan to make energy improvements to their buildings. Although we all appreciate the beauty of icicles hanging off our roof or frost on our windows, the occurrence of these two things tells us that we are wasting energy and need to make improvements to our physical plant.

The strategies in this book will guide library directors, boards, and funding sources to make small, incremental, money-saving changes in the building that will result in a leaner plant and probably serve as a model for other buildings in the community. Isn't that a great public relations tool? Just think, if you can decrease the energy consumption of your building, it will become less of a community liability and will be more likely to survive for another hundred years. Imagine offering your community an opportunity to recognize the grandeur of your building and support efforts to improve it instead of replacing it. Isn't that the most "green" thing that one can achieve?

| 1 | # PLANNING AND OTHER WORDS OF WISDOM |

MANY LIBRARIANS HAVE the skills to successfully promote their libraries through programs, events, and services. To achieve this success, we sit down with coworkers to brainstorm; after we have decided on the direction our program will take, we hash out the specific details of that program. Then we seek the support of our governing and financing bodies. We know that without this support our ideas will be less than successful. After that we work on the public relations campaign; we need our communities to turn out for the event, otherwise everything we've invested in the program is wasted. The more complicated the event, the more planning it requires. The same holds true for any building project you may embark upon.

The key to *any* successful program is *planning*. The key to *any* successful *building project*, be it large or small, lies in the *planning* process. If you have a history of winning summer reading programs, literacy projects, or Internet training classes, then *you have the skills* necessary to complete a *successful building project*.

Successful Endeavor

1. Brainstorming and conceiving an idea
2. Seeking support
3. Seeking funding
4. Hiring experts
5. Purchasing supplies and equipment
6. Public relations
7. Project completion
8. Follow-up reporting
9. Documentation
10. (Most often done on a shoestring budget!)

When solving the mystery in the newest book by our favorite author, we look to answer the questions: who, what, where, when, why, and how. When embarking on a building project we ask the same questions, along with gathering information about the return on investment and the long-term expenses that will result from the project. Although a building plan may seem overwhelming, it shouldn't be so mysterious that it is intimidating. Breaking down the project into its smaller parts by addressing the whos, whats, wheres, and whys provides an opportunity for you to look at all aspects of the project, put them down on paper, and implement the project with less anxiety.

A key question that will be asked of you, especially if you are changing to more energy-efficient equipment, involves how long it will take for that equipment to pay for itself, often called the return on investment (ROI). You will be asked to look at the cost of the equipment and how much money it promises to save you annually. Once you have these figures, you will be able to say that the new equipment will pay for itself in so many years. Let's use our heating system as an example. If you install a new state-of-the-art Energy Star furnace, you can expect to save lots of money on heating every year. For example, if it costs you $25,000 to install the new-technology furnace and you expect to save $5,000 per year in utility costs, then the equipment will pay for itself in five years, which is a great ROI. If the same technology that cost $25,000 to install only offers you an annual energy savings of $1,000, then it will take twenty-five years for the equipment to pay for itself (often the life span of the equipment), so the decision may be made that this equipment offers a poor ROI and other options should be explored. When considering the ROI, you should also ask how much it is going to cost annually to maintain the equipment. This figure should include both parts and labor. If you replace your old furnace with a new one that costs $25,000 and you expect to save $5,000 annually in heating bills, that looks great. But if you factor in the annual maintenance and upkeep for the new technology, which costs $3,000 per year for special-order parts and highly trained diagnostic service professionals, then it will take 12.5 years for the equipment to pay for itself (which is only a moderate ROI).

Thinking these things through before you begin a big project guarantees that the process from conception to final payment for work will be much smoother. Yes, unanticipated hurdles will still occur, but having a firm handle on the known factors will allow you to conserve your energy so you can deal with the ambiguity of those hurdles. It is never too early to start the planning process. If you subject all your ideas to the rigors of the process, then when you need to pull together a plan it may already exist or can be implemented with ease. The following questionnaire is a useful tool.

Example of the Planning Process

Project name [*What* is the project?]: _____

Umbrella goal [*Why* are we doing it?]: By _____, within a budget of $_____, it is hoped that the library will

    1. reduce energy consumption by $_____ or _____ percent

    2. enhance the comfort of patrons and staff

    3. address aesthetics

ROI (return on investment):

    cost of equipment / (annual savings – annual maintenance) = ROI

How we plan to do it:

    1. secure support for the project

        a.   with _____

    2. secure financing by providing realistic options and quotes

        a.   seeking grants

        b.   energy opportunities

        c.   mounting capital campaign

(cont.)

Example of the Planning Process (cont.)

3. secure material and equipment for project
4. implement the plan
5. follow up

Who is responsible

1. for developing the plan
2. for seeking support
3. for hiring experts
4. for purchasing necessary equipment and supplies
5. for actualizing the plan
6. for public relations
7. for overseeing the work
8. for decision making while work is going on
9. for documenting the effort
10. for follow-up with financial interests

What

1. experts do we need to hire
2. laborers do we need to hire
3. equipment do we need
4. needs to be moved or cordoned off to keep the collection and patrons safe
5. materials and supplies need to be brought in
6. can be borrowed or rented as opposed to purchased

Where

1. will we get the needed materials, supplies, and equipment
2. will the work be done, and how will that affect our daily operations
3. will we store all the materials and tools
4. will the workers eat lunch, park vehicles, relieve themselves, take breaks
5. will our staff do their daily activities that have been displaced

IF EVERYTHING GOES ACCORDING TO PLAN . . .

After completing the planning questionnaire, state in your own words what your goals, dreams, and aspirations are for the project. Start this *short* narrative: "If everything goes according to plan . . ." This is a great exercise because it gives you the time to sit quietly and formulate in your mind the statements you will use to promote the project. When the town reporter gets wind of your plan and shows up for an interview, you have already answered all of her questions about why you believe the project needs to be completed.

WORST-CASE SCENARIO

The final exercise you should conduct in the planning process involves thinking about the worst thing that could happen on the project and what your response would be. Concluding with a *worst-case scenario* gives you a chance to think about what might happen and address issues such as

- work that isn't completed in the scheduled time
- equipment that is installed but doesn't interface smoothly with existing infrastructure
- someone who is hurt on the job
- a contractor who doesn't show up at the appointed time
- as work is progressing, you become unhappy with the work being done

THINKING THROUGH YOUR plan from start to finish is critical. Whenever you have a job done on-site, whether it is as simple as cleaning the carpet or something as large as constructing an addition, the project will affect your building and those who use the building. When considering any work in your building, remember the butterfly effect: one small change in a system may have a considerable effect on the system at large. What you may think is a simple change in the building can lead to significant changes in the physical layout of the building, the behavior of staff and patrons, and even the library's ideology. To reduce the butterfly effect, the key to the success of your planning is getting everyone involved early on in the process. Our management classes and on-the-job experience have taught us that joint decision making increases ownership of the project, which in turn increases support for the project. If you have a broad base of support from the ground up, then your chances for a successful outcome increase significantly.

You can never overthink the planning process. When I worked on projects with my father, he used to say over and over again: "Measure twice, cut once," and "If it is off a fraction of an inch on this end, it will be a mile out of whack at the other end." Both of these practical lessons should be remembered and serve as guides when engaged in the planning process. Going through the process can be both exhilarating and excruciating. The worst-case scenario exercise will better prepare you for the project, reduce your stress level, and enhance the opportunity for a positive outcome. It is better to go through the rigors of decision making before the decisions need to be made rather than being forced to make them when every second counts.

DOCUMENTING THE PROJECT

The final component of your planning process is the documentation of the project. Aside from the paperwork from contractors and the drawings for the project, you should also group and retain three categories of paperwork, each in a separate file: funding, choices, and equipment. Communication logs should be kept in each of the three files that allow you to keep track of all conversations and decisions you make with key players throughout the process. Any documentation on expenses, grant proposals, quotes, and bills should be kept in the funding file. You may need to provide this information in reports to funding sources at a later time, so keep all this together. The second file contains information on the aesthetic choices or practical choices you have made. Include samples whenever possible, as well as information on manufacturers, vendors, colors, textures, installation dates, and cost.

The final file should contain all the equipment manuals, warranties, and provider information. It is not unreasonable to ask the installing professionals to record a short video talking about the equipment and how it works. If they are reluctant to do that, the least they should do is provide a quick step-by-step instructional guide for the operation of the equipment. If the equipment is in nonpublic areas, this information can be written right on the equipment with a waterproof marker. It is a good idea to write the installation date and the installer name right on the equipment as well. When the project is done, all these files can be boxed up for storage without much effort. You will have the knowledge that if needed, these files can be accessed quickly and easily (and trust me, you will need these files at a later date, especially when you need to buy some touch-up paint or a new carpet square).

In conclusion, we hope to give you a few ideas for increased energy efficiency but, most important, a level of confidence from a more thorough understanding of how your building works. We hope you will be better prepared to sell those ideas because of your increased comfort with and knowledge of building science. Don't look at each project as some overwhelming, gigantic monster. Instead, break it down into its smaller parts and manage it. *You have had experience* with successful programming efforts; look at your building projects the same way. Our parting words of advice to you are: "Plan for the expected, prepare for the unexpected" in all things you do in the library, from planning your next preschool storytime to building that 4,500-square-foot addition. It is all the same, just of greater magnitude.

2 | IMMEDIATE COST- SAVING MEASURES

AS MENTIONED IN the introduction, this book has been prepared to help the library professional with little or no building science knowledge better understand how a building "works." Even though both authors are life-long inhabitants of the Northeast, the concepts discussed in this book will be applicable to buildings anywhere in the country, because the goal of this work is to provide the reader with general building science knowledge. Specifically, the premise of this book, and its primary benefit, is that knowledge of your building will result in a more energy-efficient plant because you will look at your building with an eye for wasted resources and will therefore find ways to tighten up the building envelope (the outer shell of the building). The secondary benefit of this knowledge will become obvious when you are speaking with engineers, architects, and contractors and you understand what they are talking about. Finally, the tertiary benefit will be your credibility factor when you can speak confidently about your building with your board of directors, your funding sources, and your community.

Nearly 40 percent of the energy used within your building is for the operation of the heating, ventilating, and cooling equipment (HVAC).[1] It is advised that a trusted professional be hired to do a complete analysis of the efficiency of those particular systems. This professional should check that motors in your system are calibrated, that boiler igniters are clean and firing properly, and that fans and blowers are balanced.

As building managers, we can examine our facilities to look for things that are causing the HVAC systems to run harder, longer, and less effectively than they should. If you have done any research on how to make your building more energy efficient, then you have probably already made a few inexpensive and basic changes in your building. A few behavioral and physical changes will provide you with some immediate savings with little or no money invested. These changes do not require any contractors, special installation instructions, or understanding of building science; they are simply changes in habits and small hardware.

PROGRAMMABLE THERMOSTATS

- Install programmable thermostats. Cost: under $100 per thermostat. (See figures 2.1 and 2.2.)
- Buy thermostats that allow for both *weekday* and *weekend* programming (unless your hours of operation are the same for all seven days of the week).
- Buy a thermostat that allows you to program it and then lock it with a password. Use the lock feature. Don't give out the password.
- Installation is simple. Replace every old dial thermostat with a new programmable one by removing the old one and following the instructions for wiring the new one.

FIGURE 2.1
OLD THERMOSTAT

FIGURE 2.2
NEW THERMOSTAT

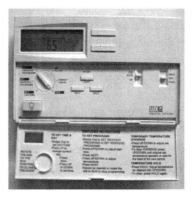

- Recommended money-saving thermostat setting: 65–67° F during the winter and 78° F for summer air-conditioning.
- Change the battery in the thermostat annually. Make it part of your tune-up routine with your heating and cooling contractor.

CEILING FANS

- Are you using your ceiling fans?[2] Ceiling fans circulate air; they don't provide any cooling relief. *You should use your ceiling fans* in the *winter* to push the warm air that rises up your ceiling down to the floor. *Run the fan on low* to do this.
- Turn on the fan. Look up. If it is *winter*, your fan should be circling in a *clockwise* direction. If it is *summer*, your fan should be circling in a *counterclockwise* direction. If it isn't, then change it. Unless you have a remote control, this will involve climbing a ladder and finding the control switch that is on the housing of the fan. *Cost-free!*
- Look up at your ceiling fan. *Is your ceiling fan flush against the ceiling?* If you have high ceilings and the fan is against the ceiling, then it will not provide you with any circulating assistance. It is using energy but not providing any benefit. Have someone come in and install an extension to bring the fan down. *Cost:* extension and installation.

WINDOWS

- Have you put your storm windows into position for the season? Are your *sash locks* in the *closed* position? Although this may seem simple, many times people close windows and never use the sash lock. If your windows are rattling in the wind, check the lock to see that it is in the closed position. Rattling windows can be an opening for cold air. This simple solution is a free and easy way to keep cold, drafty air out of your work space! If the sash locks aren't functional, then replace them.
- To keep the heat out during the summer, it is suggested that windows and doors remain closed during hot and humid weather. Open your windows at night to let the cool air in, but close them before the sun is at its hottest.
- *Window treatments:* write a *summer/winter* rule for using your window treatments. *Cost:* nothing, *behavioral change.*

- For cold climates, purchase the most energy-saving window treatments you can afford. Double or triple cellular blinds are the most energy-efficient ones.
- An alternative for warm climates is window film. Look for professional installers in your area for price quotes.

HVAC

- Have your HVAC units serviced before use each season.
- This servicing should include cleaning and/or replacing all filters. Filters should also be cleaned and/or replaced every month. Cleaning/replacing your filters allows your HVAC units to run more efficiently, because air can pass more freely through the systems. The added bonus of clean filters is fewer dust particles blowing through your environment—which means less allergens and dirt.
- Your HVAC professional will check all components of your system and guarantee that all settings are for maximum energy savings.

HOT WATER TANK

Unless you are taking showers at your library, you should consider turning *down* the temperature of your hot water tank to 105° F. The myth of hand washing was that the hotter the water the better. The Food and Drug Administration (FDA) has recently changed the recommended temperature from 120° F to 105° F. Researchers found that higher temperatures did not improve the efficacy of hand washing.[3] In fact, it was found that the tolerable temperature for washing hands was not hot enough to kill bacteria. The FDA scientists reported that hot water is more likely to cause excessive drying of the skin. It is that drying that makes it harder to remove bacteria from dry skin because of extra cracks and grooves. This, the researchers felt, would lead to painful hand washing and therefore less thorough scrubbing. As a rule, the best temperature to wash hands is the warmest temperature that you find comfortable.

ELECTRICAL APPLIANCES

Make energy-smart choices when replacing small appliances, computers, and lights and lightbulbs, as well as HVAC, roofing, windows, and window treatments.

NOTES

1. Johanna Sands, "Sustainable Library Design," AIA and Libraries Design Project, http://librisdesign.org/docs/SustainableLibDesign.pdf.
2. "Set and Save," http://changehappensindegrees.org/lookup-thermostats-fans.aspx.
3. Handwashingforlife, www.handwashingforlife.com/files/HandwashWaterv2.doc.

3 | BEGINNER BUILDING SCIENCE LESSONS

OKAY LIBRARIANS, brace yourselves, because we are going to discuss the physics of your building. Some of the concepts we know about intuitively. We remember watching our grandmother closing the windows and heavy curtains early in the morning on a hot August day and opening them after dark. We never quite understood why she did this, but we sure did enjoy sitting in her cool living room during those dog days of summer. It is the goal of this chapter to impart a little knowledge about why these old strategies make sense. If you already understand why closing the windows and window treatments works, then feel free to skip ahead. But if you don't, then buckle your seat belt and get ready for a little science.

LESSON 1: EAST, WEST, NORTH, SOUTH, AND WHAT THAT MEANS

Look at your building. Orient yourself with the equator. Start using the terms *north, south, east,* and *west* to identify the geography of your facility. Using these directional terms is the first step in understanding exactly how your building is affected by its orientation.

> ## Hint!
>
> It is easier to communicate with contractors in these terms (north, south, east, and west) instead of using the names of the rooms within your building. "The windows in the Spectacular Room need to be caulked" leaves the contractor stymied about where the job needs to be done. Whereas if you say "The windows in the northeast corner of the building need to be caulked," you are using their nomenclature and there will be an immediate understanding.

During the winter months the sun travels closer to the horizon and thus at a lower angle to your building. This means that sunlight coming in the south-facing windows on your building can provide a significant solar heat gain. On sunny winter days, open those southern window treatments and let the solar heat stream in! Keep your window treatments closed on the north, east, and west sides of your building because there is no possibility for this heat gain (and only loss, if you have large, old windows).

In the summer, the morning sun saturates the east side of your building, adding a significant amount of heat in the building. The same thing happens on the west side of your building late in the day. Ideally, there are shade trees or exterior awnings on your building to help alleviate some of the solar heat gain. If not, keep your window treatments closed to block some of this heat. Because the sun is at its highest in the sky during the summer, solar heat gain through southern windows is minimal, so you can again use these windows to let natural light in without a significant heat gain.

LESSON 2: HEAT TRANSFER

Heat transfer is simply the movement of heat in your building.

Winter → Heat Moves from Indoors to Outdoors
Summer → Heat Moves from Outdoors to Indoors

There are three mechanisms by which heat transfer occurs: *conduction, convection,* and *radiation*. Conduction is the direct transfer of heat from particle to particle in or between substances. Convection is the transfer of heat by the movement of warm matter in a gas or liquid, as in the flow of warm currents in air. Radiation is the third force acting on your building. Radiation is the transfer of energy through space without the aid of fluids or solids. The primary example of radiation is sunlight, which transports energy through both the vacuum of space and the gases of the atmosphere.

Think of these three mechanisms as you sit around a campfire cooking a pot of beans. Convection is the process whereby the heat of the fire is transferred to your beans, warming them to your liking. You experience conduction when you burn your hand on the handle of the pot, which is too hot to touch. Radiation is how you feel sitting around the fire. On a cold night the side facing the fire is warm, but the side facing away from the fire is cold. Let's use our favorite beverage as another example of how heat is transferred. Conduction occurs when we have a spoon resting in our cup of hot coffee. The spoon absorbs the heat from the coffee, and it warms to the touch. Let's take this a step further. If you think of your building on a hot summer day, the hot air outside warms the walls of the building, and these walls in turn warm the air inside the building. The heat is transferred through the walls by means of conduction.

A popular misconception is that heat rises. Heat actually flows through solid materials toward the cold in every direction. We may think that the cold air is moving into our hot cup of coffee at the annual Christmas book sale, but that is not true. The difference in the temperature between the hot coffee and the cold air causes the cold air to pull the energy (i.e., heat) from the cup of coffee, thus cooling it more quickly. The greater the difference between the two temperatures, the faster this happens. Using an insulated mug stems the effects of conduction, or what is called conductive heat loss.

Understanding convection, or how heat moves through the air in your building, means you understand that there is a balance between the inside and outside temperatures and how those differences affect that balance. Your building is waging a constant battle between hot and cold air, and who wins the battle depends on the inside/outside temperature and the presence of leaks that allow one force an advantage over another, depending on the season. The movement of air into and out of your building is known as the stack effect.

To better understand this concept, let us assume that your building is covered with a giant garbage bag. Let us also assume that there are 100 pounds of air in your building. If the temperature outside is 65° F and the temperature inside is 65° F, the difference is zero. This means your building is under a constant pressure, and the 100 pounds of air remain at rest. During the winter the inside of your building is 65° F and the outside temperature is 10° F. The difference between the two temperatures is 55° F. The warm air in the building rises to the top of the interior space, causing an increase in pressure there and reducing the pressure in the lower levels of the building. The warm air escapes through windows or other leaks to the outside, allowing cold outside air to infiltrate the lower levels of the building. So the 100 pounds of air are made up of more cold air than hot, and your furnace works overtime to heat the cold air. If you stood outside your building that is covered with a garbage bag, you would see that it balloons out at the top of the building. Think of it as all your heated air trying to escape through the roof.

Remember:
HOT air = LIGHT air
COLD air = HEAVY air

During the summer, the inside temperature of your air-conditioned building is 75° F and the outside temperature is 95° F. The difference between these two temperatures is –20° and means that your building is in a state of low pressure. The superheated air from your attic is drawn down by the cool air in the lower levels and displaces the cool air, which leaks out through the openings of the lower levels. If you looked at your building from the outside, the giant garbage bag that is over your building would balloon out at the bottom of the building. Or in this case, the 100 pounds of air in your building are made up of more hot air than cool, so your air conditioners must work harder trying to cool the hot air that is being pulled down through your building.

Although conduction has to do with the movement of heat or cold through the walls of our buildings, and convection describes the movement of hot and cold air within our buildings, it is solar heat that affects our true level of comfort most directly, especially if we are in a room with lots of windows. It is for this reason we use blinds, shades, or curtains to block the unwanted rays of the sun from entering through windows during the summer, and we allow sunlight to enter the windows in the cold of winter.

During the winter the radiation, sometimes called solar or thermal heat, that comes through your southern windows warms the room and feels good, while during the summer the thermal heat that comes through your windows is more intense and feels more uncomfortable. Think of your cat. On a cold winter day the cat can probably be found sitting in the sunbeams soaking up the heat, purring away and sleeping soundly. On a hot day, the same cat would probably enjoy the warm feeling for only a short period of time before growing uncomfortable and seeking the cooling comfort of the porcelain bathtub or a dark corner of your room. The same holds true for humans in our buildings.

<table>
<tr><td>4</td><td># KNOW THY BUILDING:
WHAT IS INSIDE</td></tr>
</table>

BEFORE WE GO any further, take a moment to answer the following questions:

1. Do you know how much electricity your building uses on a monthly basis? Historically over the last five, ten, or twenty years?

2. Do you know what type of fuel is used to run your heating systems? Heating oil, natural gas, propane, steam, geothermal, electric?

3. Do you know how much of that fuel your building uses on a monthly basis? Historically over the last five, ten, or twenty years?

4. Do you know where the service shutoffs are located in your building? Water, electric, fuel?

5. Do you have or know where to get the original blueprints of your building, as well as blueprints for any additional construction projects?

6. Do you know the age of your furnace, boiler, hot water tank, and roofing shingles?

If you answered "Yes" to these questions, you are well aware of how your building works. If you answered "No," then it is time to do some research into your old utility bills and spend some time getting to know your plant.

IT SURE MAKES YOU LOOK GOOD IF YOU KNOW YOUR NUMBERS . . .

The first step to knowing your building is having the information available to you that allows for seasonal and annual analysis. If you don't have the old bills, then check with your utility companies. They often keep a record of your bills for the previous eighteen to twenty-four months and will give you a nicely summarized report. Create a spreadsheet in whichever application you use. Save the spreadsheet to your desktop as "utilities usage." Break it down by service category: electric, heating fuel, and, if you are metered, water. It is imperative that you make a habit of recording this data every month when you receive your utility bills. At a minimum, your spreadsheet should contain data on (1) billed demand, (2) daily average use, (3) number of service days, (4) monthly charge, and (5) average temperature for the billing cycle. All this information should appear on each bill you receive, especially from your larger utility services.

Your job as the manager of the library requires you to keep track of all your expenses. Just as you record your acquisition and other operational expenses, recording the data from your utility bills every month needs to become part of your regular accounting. Having these utility spreadsheets at your disposal will help you in several ways. The data will allow you to quickly identify any problems with your HVAC equipment, because if your furnace or air-conditioning system isn't functioning properly, you will see a gigantic increase in the amount of energy it takes to run it. It may take a billing cycle to see this, but the situation can be quickly remedied by a call to your HVAC service; this is much better than running an entire season inefficiently.

Spreadsheets with all of the key information about utility usage, when combined with information pertaining to the average monthly outside temperature, provide valuable information on seasonal abnormalities. For example, in January 2009 we were quite upset because our building consumed more No. 2 heating oil than had been projected. We watched our prepaid heating-fuel account dwindle quickly, and we were especially upset because this was happening despite the energy-saving measures we had completed prior to the start of the heating season. Our concern was alleviated when we received our electric bill. While inputting the data, we quickly noted that the January of concern was almost 9° colder than the previous three Januarys. It was actually the coldest month of which we had a record. Armed with this information, we were able to justify the extra gallons of heating oil it took to keep our old building warm, and we felt consolation in knowing that if we hadn't insulated and used our new energy-efficient double cellular blinds, then the amount of heating oil we used would have been much more. (See figure 4.1.)

These statistics also come in handy when preparing budgets and presenting them at budget hearings. It is nearly impossible to argue against the numbers—especially if you have documented reductions in your use of the utilities. For example, during the summer of 2007 we used 11,076 kilowatt-hours (KWH) of electricity. During the summer of 2008 we used 8,847 KWH of electricity. The library decreased its consumption by 2,229 KWH of electricity, yet our bill for the three-month period was only $118 less than the same months of the prior year. (See figure 4.2.) The reality of the high cost

FIGURE 4.1
HEATING OIL TRACKING

2007–2008 HEATING SEASON; PRICE PER GALLON $2.49

PAID	ACCOUNT BALANCE	DELIVERY DATE	GALLONS DELIVERED
	$3,498.60		
$55.48	$3,443.12	10/25/2007	22
$257.40	$3,185.72	11/27/2007	103
$353.86	$2,831.86	12/13/2007	141.6
$257.40	$2,728.86	12/24/2007	103
$315.37	$2,413.49	1/9/2008	126.2
$263.14	$2,150.35	1/24/2008	105.3
$224.16	$1,926.19	2/4/2008	89.7
$383.10	$1,543.09	2/20/2008	153.3
$381.35	$1,161.74	3/6/2008	152.6
$238.65	$923.09	3/19/2008	95.5
$328.87	$594.22	4/7/2008	131.6
$286.86	$307.36	5/19/2008	114.8
			1,493

of energy prompted the board of trustees to look at larger projects that would have a greater impact on the overall energy consumption of our library. The question became: what more could we do?

YOUR BUILDING: SHUTOFFS, SWITCHES, AND MAPS

It is critical to know where the main service shutoffs are located in your building and to make sure that they are easily accessible. This means that old surplus supplies should not be stacked in front of the access areas. This means that all those old books you are storing for your book sale need to be moved out of the corner where your water main shutoff is located. The time it takes for you or emergency personnel to find and get to those shutoffs can be critical. For example, if you have a water leak on the top floor, the sooner it is discovered and the water is turned off, the less damage your building will suffer. If it takes you ten minutes to find the shutoff and another five minutes moving surplus equipment so you can get to the shutoff, you now have a major disaster on your hands. If someone reports the smell of gas or oil in your building or your carbon monoxide detectors are alarming, your first order of business is to immediately evacuate the building. Once outside, use your cell phone or a neighbor's phone to call 911. If there is gas in your building, any small electrical charge can set off an explosion. Do not attempt to shut off any service yourself. Do not turn anything off. Your job is to wait for properly trained emergency personnel to arrive. Then you will need to tell them exactly where the gas or oil shutoff is located. Chances are, they will also ask for the location of the electric service shutoff. This is why it is imperative that your library have a working disaster plan.

A high-quality disaster plan should include copies of your building blueprint or, at the very least, floor plans with all the critical services marked. During an emergency, as you are leaving or coming into the building, make sure you grab your copy of the disaster plan. Your binder should include multiple copies of the building layout, so all emergency personnel who need the information will have it available to them. The layout should be broken down by floor and should include the locations of all fire equipment and service shutoffs, as well as the location of keys for access to locked areas.

To become more familiar with your building, it would be a good idea to take the floor plans with you on a monthly inspection. As you do your walk-through, make notes on the floor plan of problems, issues, or concerns you discover. Make certain that all your fire extinguishers are in the locations as marked and that they all have their clips in place. Look at the windows in your

FIGURE 4.2
ELECTRICITY TRACKING

READ DATE	BILLED DEMAND	USAGE	NO. DAYS	USAGE/ DAY	CHARGE	AVE. TEMP.
Jan-08	10.90	2,064	29	71.17	$311.41	23.20
Feb-08	10.60	2,340	30	78.00	$337.51	25.90
Mar-08	10.60	2,280	29	78.62	$331.27	30.70
Apr-08	10.30	2,340	32	73.12	$334.91	45.50
May-08	10.30	2,436	31	78.58	$344.90	54.00
Jun-08	23.20	2,604	27	96.44	$474.20	66.40
Jul-08	22.20	3,348	33	101.45	$576.76	71.20
Aug-08	21.40	2,892	30	96.40	$518.69	67.00
Sep-08	21.20	2,628	32	82.13	$487.49	62.30
Oct-08	10.20	2,160	30	72.00	$335.31	48.40
Nov-08	10.70	2,136	30	71.20	$337.19	38.30
Dec-08	10.30	1,920	32	60.00	$309.44	28.00
Jan-09	9.70	1,968	29	68.00	$322.24	14.80
Feb-09	10.20	2,028	30	68.00	$334.47	23.00
Mar-09	8.50	1,752	28	62.57	$286.00	31.00
Apr-09	8.90	1,908	32	59.63	$308.14	46.00
May-09	9.40	2,040	31	65.81	$328.39	55.00
Jun-09	18.00	1,836	28	65.57	$384.84	62.00
Jul-09	19.10	2,256	32	70.50	$444.65	65.00
Aug-09	20.60	3,708	31	119.61	$633.23	70.00

building for signs of weathering, tampering, or aging. Change the filters in your furnace. Make sure all your service shutoffs are easily accessible. If you have alarms on emergency exits, make sure those alarms are working and that all stairwells, hallways, or egresses are clear of clutter and are accessible.

KNOWING THE VITAL DATA OF YOUR EQUIPMENT: AN ABSOLUTE NECESSITY

Your final assignment is to create a spreadsheet containing information about all your vital equipment. This vital equipment includes your heating, air-conditioning, hot water tank, boiler, humidifiers, dehumidifiers, windows, and roofing. Include the manufacturer, model number, serial number, service contacts, and age of the equipment. (See figure 4.3.) If you don't know the age of the equipment, a call to the manufacturer with a model number or serial number will enable them to tell you when the equipment was manufactured. (This will give you the approximate age of the equipment, but it doesn't tell you how long it has been in service in your building.) As you get new equipment, make it a habit to write this information on the equipment itself, along with any special operating instructions on the equipment, and finally record this information on your spreadsheet. Record the location of this equipment on your floor plan or layout. Print this spreadsheet on the back of the layout for your disaster plan. You should have received an operations and maintenance manual with your new equipment. The installer should also have arranged training for your maintenance team on the equipment as well. Remember that you will have at least a one-year warranty on the equipment. Record the date you have accepted the equipment, so you know when you need to start paying for any repairs. If you don't have an experienced maintenance team, be sure to arrange for a service contract on all your expensive equipment.

Having all this data at your fingertips will help you not only in an emergency but also when planning building improvements. If your funding source requires a schedule of capital improvement projects, you can confidently lay out your plans. If you know exactly how old the furnace is, your HVAC professional can provide you with the approximate utilization expectancy for that particular model. If your furnace is 15 years old and its utilization expectancy is 25 years, you can rest assured that barring any major system failure, you have 10 more years in which to plan for your next heating source. If you know the roof is 25 years old and the life span of the shingles is only 20 years, then you may need to move that project up on your to-do list.

FIGURE 4.3
RECURRING MAINTENANCE LIST

EQUIPMENT	MANUFACTURER'S NAME	MODEL # OR SERIAL #	YEAR OF INSTALLATION	MAINTAINED BY	CONTACT PERSON	PHONE, ROUTINE SERVICE	PHONE, EMERGENCIES
Boiler	Weil	2344456684	1998	ABC Plumbing	Sally Francis	123-4566	123-4566
Furnace	Austin	2223584398	2005	HW HVAC	John Smith	234-5678	550-5555
Air Conditioner	Smith	9910999135	2000	HW HVAC	John Smith	234-5678	550-5555

As information professionals, we know that knowledge is power. Spending the time getting to know the intricacies of your building means there will be fewer surprises and you will be fighting fewer fires. Instead of scrambling for funds to pay for an emergency replacement of your fifty-year-old furnace, you can approach the project incrementally. Your funding source and your governing body will thank you for having the foresight to gather this information and will work with you to plan for the replacement of these critical building components.

<table>
<tr><td>5</td><td># WHAT YOUR BUILDING SITS ON AND WHY</td></tr>
</table>

WHAT YOUR BUILDING SITS ON AND WHY

YOUR BUILDING IS part of a larger picture. When you are considering your building, you have to think beyond the four walls. Your structure includes not only the building but its plumbing, windows, utility services, roof, and what the building is sitting on, that is, the earth. When town centers were being settled, the builders had their choice of optimal building sites. They selected sites where the soil was stable, dry, and probably not subject to recurring flooding. The depth of the hole that was dug for your building's foundation depended on the characteristics of the soil in your area, as well as your location. In this chapter we will explore why this is important to occupants of old buildings.

Soils need to have certain characteristics to be considered good for building. Your structure should sit on dirt or crushed rock, ideally of mixed particle size without the presence of organic materials, which is referred to as loam. Loam contains organic substances that are in a state of decomposition. If your building is in a loamy area, then the builders took extra care to compensate for the loam so your building wouldn't shift and settle as the loam does what it is supposed to do: decompose as nutrients for the earth.

Depending on your location, your soil may be composed of crushed rock, crushed seashells, or sand. The best soil will consist of a mix of particle sizes. Many call this gravel, a broken rock from the glaciers that swept the northern regions. This is an ideal material because of its angular nature, with its sharp edges and uneven faces. With these characteristics, the pieces lock together. The smaller pieces fill the spaces, so you don't have a lot of open voids. Thus, settlement is eliminated.

If your building is on solid rock, you won't ever need to worry about settlement, but you will certainly feel any small earthquake. If your building is on rock, you can be sure the foundation cost was high. To build your structure below the frost line, the construction crew had to blast through the rock to dig the foundation hole. Once they excavated the hole they had to address what your building would be sitting on, or the ledge, as it's called in the trade. Most times the ledge isn't even, so to level it, soil is placed back on top of the rock. Care must be taken when backfilling the ledge because the soil that is used for leveling may contain a lot of moisture, and if it isn't below the frost line, it will freeze.

WHAT'S ALL THIS TALK ABOUT FROST AND WHY DON'T WE LIKE IT?

When it gets cold out, down to about 25° F, the ground freezes. This means that any moisture in the soil freezes. This water in the ground has the nasty habit of expanding when it freezes. The ground then lifts everything above it and breaks things, including our foundations. In the spring, when the ground thaws out, the earth and everything on top of it goes down again. It is this freeze-thaw cycle that causes damage to our foundations, cement pads, and any other structure that has not been designed to accommodate the shifting of the earth. This is why it is imperative to build below where the soil freezes each winter, or as it is called in the building trades, "below the frost line." In the Northeast, this depth is approximately four feet below the surface — colder areas require deeper foundation holes — while in the South the depth is much shallower.

The combination of a well-designed foundation hole and materials that are indigenous to your building area results in a building that is not affected by the weather. The contractors who built your structure looked for the characteristics of a good building site: good-quality soil that drains well and is above the seasonal high water table. These can be considered frost-free soils. These soils don't hold any water, and any water that does get in drains off, so it's never there to freeze. Rest assured that if you are in an old building, the contractors who built your structure took great care to address these issues. However, small changes in your area can greatly affect your building, and that is why a little soil/environmental knowledge goes a long way in protecting the integrity of your building and saving you from major repair bills.

WHY WORRY IF YOU HAVE AN OLD BUILDING?

Soil frost and bearing issues can come into play even if you have a classic old building. Changes, big or small, in the land around your building may affect the integrity of the building and its structural foundation. Anytime the land around you is put to a new use, your building becomes vulnerable. You immediately become involved in a new building process. If the town decides to sell the quaint wooded lot next to your building to a franchised company that will build a new chain restaurant with a parking lot around it, you need to worry. Or if the old town hall next door is removed and a new one with a deeper foundation or a new parking lot is designed, you need to worry. If the land next to you used to be a hill and is being turned into a ball field, you need to worry.

WHAT CAN THESE SCENARIOS DO TO YOUR BUILDING?

The first thing to worry about, and the easiest problem to solve at the beginning of a new project, is the grading of the new construction. *Grading* is defined as the smoothing out of the soils to a level surface. Whoever is "developing" (a word used to describe a substantial change to the land) the project next door usually has a legal requirement to hire a licensed engineer to develop a plan for the new work. In developing the plan, they have the legal obligation not to change the drainage characteristics of your property. This is a fancy way of saying they can't design something that sends more water onto your land than what currently goes there.

That is fine if it is done properly. Hopefully, whoever issues building permits in your municipality has the authority to require the developer to meet all laws and codes. The most critical information that you need to be aware of is the designed flow parameters. The designers plug the parameters into software packages that model water flow after rain events. The heavier the rainfall numbers they put into the model, the more flow the design has to accommodate. This means bigger pipes, bigger detention pods, and of course more cost. It is important that you have a qualified advocate for your building looking at the plans before the developer is allowed to proceed. You need to have a guarantee that the numbers they are using are adequate, or else the project will be underdesigned and could therefore significantly alter the drainage characteristics of your property and compromise the integrity of your building's foundation.

LATERAL SUPPORT

Another issue to be concerned about is when developers put in a deeper foundation next to your building. They are going to dig a big hole, and depending on the soil the hole may actually undermine your building. A little structural engineering with soil-bearing science is in order here. Soil is loaded vertically. Because it is granular, it takes this load but doesn't deliver it all straight down. Because the particles are round, they transfer the load to wherever the soil grains are touching the next grains. The maximum angle at which this transfer takes place is a function of the soils your building is sitting on. If the soil consists of round particles, there is no way they can lock on to each other, so they will fall away when someone digs next to them. If the particles have an irregular, angular shape and are of different sizes, they can lock on to each other and will not fall away when support from the sides is removed. With the right soil mix you can dig straight down, and the hole will stay open. With loose soils, the particles will slope away up to 45 degrees. This is called the angle of repose. The looser the soil, the greater the angle of repose. The smaller the variation in the size of the soil particles (i.e., the more uniform they are), the higher the angle of repose and the farther the effect reaches. Picture straight down as 0 degrees; as you move from the vertical, the angle of repose becomes greater as the soils become loose (90 degrees would be like being in mud, while 0 degrees is like being on rock). Many designers and contractors will go in assuming an angle of 45 degrees and see where the actual soil is. So when you have loose soils, your neighbor had better be as far away from you as the distance they are planning to dig down to ensure your building won't be undermined.

Contractors are required to comply with many federal regulations. Occupational Safety and Health Administration standards require the contractor to know how loose the soil is before they start digging. Once they have this information, they are required to provide a safe work setting for their employees. The contractor is also required to have someone on-site who is trained and responsible for the safety of the workers. This person has the title of "competent person." Anytime there is digging occurring, the competent person must be on the site. There are other aspects of the work that also require a competent person, but with different skill requirements.

The developer looks at soil information when they are designing the foundation. Part of their obligation is to know how and if your building will be affected or placed at risk. As a neighbor, you may never know how the new design will affect your building, but they are required to design a building that does no harm to neighboring property. This design would incorporate shoring or a list of limits for the excavation. If someone comes to you with a building plan that involves shoring your building, this means they want to drive sheeting or drill anchors under your building to anchor everything. They must have your permission to do this. To protect yourself you should have a copy of their insurance, and they need to have a big policy written to protect your building if this work needs to be done.

YOUR OWN NEW SMALLER PROJECTS

You may find you have a small project to do that will involve consideration of soil issues. The most common mistakes made in the soil and site area occur when you put in a new entry, have a new ADA ramp put in, or change the landscaping of your building.

THE OUTSIDE PAD

If you are putting in a new entry or ramp, remember that you must dig below the frost line for your area and put a foundation in under your pad. If you do not, our friend Mr. Frost will push your pad up and your door will not open. This is especially critical if there are stairs involved. The cantilevered action of the lifting of the stairs in a frost situation could lift your pad many inches. Don't skimp. Even for the smallest job, if it is suggested you put in a foundation — *put in a foundation.*

THE NEW LAWN AND PLANTINGS

If you have the opportunity to put in a new lawn, be certain of a couple of things. First, be sure the final grade is below your first floor. If you have a masonry building, the grade can't be higher than the weeps, the little holes in the brick that allow water out. This is usually the bottom brick, but not always. If you have a wood building, *never bury the wood — not even treated wood.* It's still wood. If wood is moist, it will rot and dissolve.

EARTHQUAKES

How your building reacts to an earthquake is pretty much dependent on what type of soil it is sitting on. To understand what an earthquake does, imagine your building sitting all by itself on a table. Now push the table. The force of your push mimics the earthquake. Your building moves a little. If you have soft soil, it will want to move too, sometimes faster and more than your building. This can affect the soil's bearing capacity and change it for an instant, the instant that the force is being applied. In extreme conditions, your building will settle to a new condition and not be level. In the case of a severe quake, the soil may act like water and simply liquefy. When this happens your building can actually sink. The biggest problem, and the one that will cause most of the damage, is when your building is pushed at the very bottom and the top has to play catch-up. Unfortunately, your building was designed for the top part to sit on the lower part. The two parts don't act the same in the case of an earthquake, and the result is that the building gets whiplashed. Then, as your building experiences typical post-earthquake tremors and aftershocks, the whiplashing occurs over and over again, and the structural integrity of the building is jeopardized.

As the occupant of an old building, what should you look to do in case of an earthquake? From the soils aspect, there is really nothing to be done. Geotechnical factors and plate tectonics pretty much define the hazards you face. Suffice it to say that if your building is in sand, the force will be less than if it is on a ledge, but settlement is more of a concern. If your building sits on clay soils or has piles or a deep foundation, there is a lot more to be concerned about but nothing that you can really do.

<table>
<tr><td>6</td><td></td></tr>
</table>

6   THE FOUNDATION

ONCE IT IS determined what kind of ground or soil is at a construction site, a builder or engineer is hired to design the building. Even though the foundation is the first thing built, it is usually one of the last components of the building designed. The foundation is determined by the shape and purpose of the building. The role of the foundation is critical. It absorbs all the load of the building and distributes the load to the soil surrounding the foundation.

The type of foundation designed depends on the type of soil. The simplest and most common design is the *spread footing* foundation. With this foundation all the outside walls and some of the inside walls are considered *bearing walls*. The bearing walls support the weight of the roof and floor loads. These bearing walls in turn sit on the foundation wall, which absorbs the entire weight of the building. The foundation wall sits on a wider but less deep section of the footing. If the soil is soft, the bottom of the foundation wall is wider and the foundation only has to be deep enough to be below the frost line. The same holds true if the foundation is built on a ledge, with gravelly soil on top of the ledge.

If there is clay or another deep organic stratum, *piles* might be driven to a designed depth. What does it mean to drive piles? A giant crane, which acts as a large hammer, is brought to the construction site. The hammer is actually a one-cylinder diesel engine that sits on top of the pile and hammers the pile down into the ground until a predetermined depth is reached. This depth was decided by engineers. They use an equation that takes into consideration the weight of the hammer, the contact areas of the sides of the pile, and the distance the pile goes down per blow. The results of this calculation reflect the depth the pile has to reach in order to provide adequate bearing capacity. Once the pile is in place, additional piles are driven. Finally, the piles are filled with reinforcing steel and concrete and are covered.

Another foundation technique similar to pile driving is the caisson method. If the caisson method is used, the builders aren't hammering a pile into the ground; instead, they are drilling a hole and then filling it. In the caisson method, a hole is drilled with a large auger to a designed and predetermined depth. If the soil is solid, a rebar cage is dropped into the hole and filled with concrete. Think of these as underground columns. If the soil is too soft and keeps falling into the hole, a slurry is added to the hole. The slurry has the same weight as the soil but is lighter than concrete. When the auger reaches the desired depth, the rebar cage is dropped into the hole with the slurry. Then the concrete is poured into the hole and this displaces the slurry. The slurry makes this a very complicated process and requires highly skilled crews who are basically building something without benefit of seeing throughout the process.

In the classic old building you probably won't find a lot of concrete in the foundation. Very likely your foundation was made with stone. The stones could be fieldstone, broken or cut rock, or large slabs of stone. These all have the same characteristics of the concrete we use today. The strength of this stone is 3,000 or 4,000 or more pounds per square inch. Our common concrete is 3,000 pounds per square inch. This capacity is way beyond the strength needed to support the building. This strength is necessary to support the constant load of your building over time. The building itself can affect the foundation.

Other forces on the foundation come from the outside. Thermal loading happens when you have typical northern weather. Temperatures of –10°, –20°, or –30° in the winter and then up to 90° in the summer can really put a lot of stress on the material. All material expands and contracts with temperature changes. The building design has to accommodate this. If there is no room for expansion, the material will break apart. Building corners themselves do lots of this. They actually push out or pull in when there are temperature changes.

Another powerful force on the foundation is hydrostatic pressure. If you have a basement slab with cracks in the middle, and water that flows up through the cracks, you are seeing the action of hydrostatic pressure. A lot of damage can be done to the foundation wall by hydrostatic pressure. If a new wall is built or you excavate in areas around your foundation, care must be taken when you backfill the hole. If water gets into the clay or the fill, it will expand when it freezes and will push against your wall until the wall gives out.

To avoid this, the original builder should have and probably did use a gravelly, well-drained material or installed a drainpipe at the base of the wall. This only works if you can run the drain to daylight, that is, to a point lower than the foundation for natural drainage. You don't want to use an electrically driven pump. Over time it will fail and be forgotten. If the water doesn't drain, you have what is called a bathtub. Water will sit against the wall, and it will come in through your foundation. In the classic old buildings, the owners and the builders knew this and even accepted it as the reality of building. Their design allowed water in but also provided a route for it to leave. The rooms will always be wet, musty, and damp, however. Not a good environment for much practical use.

There can be a lot of effort and expense in dealing with water entering a building through the foundation. The best efforts involve an insulating and waterproofing membrane on the exterior of the foundation, because this keeps heat inside the building and keeps groundwater out of it.

7 | THE UNDERGROUND STUFF

THE DIRT, CONCRETE, and stone aren't the only important aspects of your building that you are hopefully never going to see. Let's talk about the underground pipes. What kind of pipes do you have, and what do you need that comes through those pipes? Let's consider the electricity, the water, sewer, gas, data, phone, and Internet lines, a fire alarm line, and maybe site drainage. The lines could be just for your building, or maybe they're part of a network and they run across your property. Even though you may know where the lines come into your building, you must call a safe dig company before doing any excavating on your property.

If you have bathrooms, you have a classic case of what goes in must come out; in this case, you have water coming in and sewage going out. The water may come from a well or a municipal water system. If you are on a municipal water system, your use is probably metered so the utility can accurately charge for your use. The sewage isn't metered; they charge you based on your water bill. If you don't use a municipal system for your sewage, you may have your own leach field; in that case, there is no local bill, but be ready when the field needs replacing. The neighbors will let you know when it's time. A good field should easily last twenty years.

If you have a true classic old building, your water pipes may actually be wood. Really old wood. Rumor has it that some of Boston's water supply still comes through wood pipes. If wood is kept wet, it doesn't rot. It is more likely, however, that clay or cast-iron pipes bring in your water. During the 1960s a material called transite was used for water pipes. It was hard, and like cement, it didn't rot. After some serious lawsuits about certain mined materials in many building products, this material became unavailable. But it is still in use. They don't replace water pipes for product recalls. Today, builders use cement-lined ductile iron pipe and copper. Copper is really expensive but is impervious to the material found in water. It isn't impervious to the material found in soils, so it isn't used outside. The cement-lined ductile pipe can bend with the loads the exterior environment can put on it. Because it is cement-lined it doesn't rust too fast.

Your main electric lines may come into your building underground. It's a lot safer in many cases. The electrical pipe is called conduit and is made of galvanized steel. The wires are either copper or aluminum. Your data may come in underground too. Old phone and cable lines may be copper, while newer lines are called fiber optic, a sort of plastic.

Hopefully you will never be concerned with these underground pipes. But anytime you are working on your site and that work involves digging or cutting through your basement slab, you must take legally obligated measures to protect the lines coming in, thereby protecting the people working on your site.

1. Many states require by law that the contractor have a survey conducted of the area by the local utilities. They are required to mark all their pipes and lines. In New England this is called "Dig Safe," and it is a free service available to all contractors.

2. If the contractor is digging inside your building, he must have experts on-site who have researched the building, are aware of what could happen, and know what to do if something goes wrong. A competent contractor will shut off power before using a saw to cut a slab. This could save a life if the saw hits a high-energy power line in the concrete. This can easily happen.

If you have natural gas, it comes from a pipe in the street. Nowadays they use bright yellow plastic pipes, but if you have an old service, then you will most likely find yellow-coated steel pipes. This pipe will join to a meter on the outside of your building. After interfacing with the meter, the gas pipe converts to smaller copper pipes that transport gas to the units in your building. Natural gas burns cleanly and is therefore a very efficient fuel. The cost of natural gas is less because it doesn't involve all the trucking costs of propane or No. 2 heating oil. Natural gas is safe. The gas companies add a scent to the product, so if you have a gas leak you can smell it immediately. If you smell gas, the gas company and local fire department are very responsive and don't waste time when responding to complaints. Oil spills are a whole different story. If you have an oil spill, this becomes an environmental cleanup that may involve the demolition of what got spilled on. Propane is pretty much the same story as natural gas, except that the tank is on-site and hopefully near your boilers.

Drainage pipes are usually concrete and will be out in your parking lot. Their basic function is to take the storm water and send it to the river. Unfortunately, any grease, oil, or contaminant goes with the water. This is a violation of environmental protection laws. As such, you will often see logos stamped on the rims of the pipes noting that they drain to a protected public body of water. If you knowingly add a contaminant to the drainage pipes, you stand to face large fines imposed by your municipal sewer authority.

8 | THE STRUCTURE

SO FAR WE have learned about where your building sits, what it sits on, and the services that come into your building. The next important component we will look at is your building's walls and roof and what they are made of. What do you have sitting on that well-engineered, strong, stable foundation and fed by those reliable utilities? Your building! The structural engineers take the visionary ideas of the architects and, working within the parameters of the desired materials, make the building possible. Whether they're made of masonry, wood, or steel, the walls and roof of your building provide shelter, support, and hopefully an aesthetically pleasing centerpiece for your town.

MASONRY

Masonry walls can be made of cement block, brick, or stone. Many structures are constructed using masonry because it is easy to build with, and in the old days masonry was the most available material to use for building. Aside from the strategic location of reinforcing steel at critical parts of the block, the masonry structure is pretty much the same throughout. Every wall can be strong enough to hold whatever it needs to. Inside or out, the masonry wall looks pretty much the same. The tricky part comes when dealing with the exterior of the masonry wall. If not done correctly, you will have a wet building that is poorly insulated. You may also have a building with an attached facade, which becomes very dangerous in the event of an earthquake or deterioration. The block will have special details at certain places to make it a very strong structure. Some of the cells (the holes in the block) will be filled with a loose cement mixture called grout. They will have reinforcing steel in them. Each layer of bricks or blocks is called a course. The top courses will be filled with concrete and steel. This band ties the wall together, making it very strong. This course is called a bond beam. You will also find bond beams over your doors, windows, and all other openings. They are solid. If you need to punch a small hole through the wall for a new electrical circuit, a bond beam isn't the place to do it.

Let's look at how a properly constructed masonry wall is built. (See figure 8.1.) Let's assume the outside is brick. (This sounds simple, but the details of

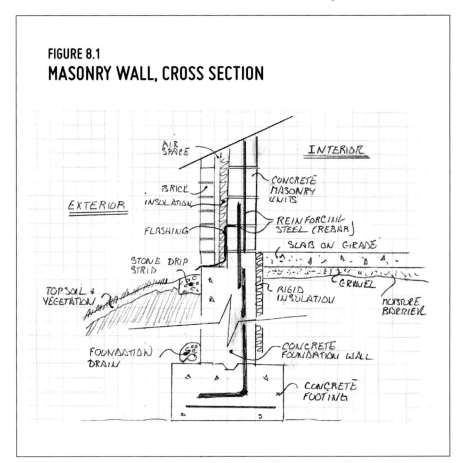

FIGURE 8.1
MASONRY WALL, CROSS SECTION

constructing a proper masonry wall have taken generations to get right, and issues of heat transfer, moisture control, and the longevity of materials have added complexity to the process.)

COMPOSITION OF A MASONRY WALL

1. Inside of the block = interior wall

2. Outside of the block = exterior wall

3. Outside of the block = *tempered area*: this is where heat loss and heat gain are controlled

4. *Tempered area*: external water can never breach this line

5. *Vapor barrier*: guarantees that water moves away from the building

6. *Insulation*

7. *Cavity*: the major purpose of this cavity is to keep the environment on the outside of the building away from the inside wall. With the cavity, the cold won't transmit through a solid; the water won't pass right through. If the cavity is too narrow, however, water will get through the brick, jump the cavity, and seep through the insulation and vapor barrier, thus getting into your building.

8. *Brick*: brick is really thick and really hard; it looks good and protects the outside wall from the elements. In newer buildings, when brick is used as the exterior facade, it is neither structural nor considered a complete weather barrier and is basically acting as paint.

Although brick buildings are easy to maintain and beautiful, great thought and planning went into the small details of using brick. For example, the detailing of the brick around windows is crucial. Because water likes to wrap around openings (e.g., window frames), extra effort was expended to guarantee that the windows are in fact waterproof. The blocks over the doors and windows have this detail too. If you are considering cutting a door in a block building, be aware that you will need to cut more than the door opening to make it structurally adequate. It's a bit of a trick for the mason to cut the hole wide enough without the building coming down, but with shoring and small needle beams they do it well. Bond beams here are limited to relatively short spans, but you may find some steel beams in your building that span larger rooms or wider openings.

STEEL

Most new buildings today have some steel in them. You can think of steel buildings in two categories: pre-engineered or structural. You probably don't have a pre-engineered building. These buildings are made of low-cost steel supports and wrinkled sheet metal for the exterior walls and roofs. Pre-engineered buildings are good for big storage sheds or gyms but are seldom used for anything like a library. Structural steel is a good economical choice for almost any type of building. It takes care of all the load requirements in a very small area, leaving the bulk of the wall line free for openings or wide-open spaces.

Steel buildings go up pretty fast, but it takes months of preparation and off-site production before the steel actually arrives at the site. A steel detailer draws up plans for the steel based on the structural engineers and architectural drawings. The detailer's drawings are made to show the team in the steel shop exactly what steel shapes to buy, what lengths to cut and weld them, and where to put the holes for bolting it all together. When the steel arrives on-site, it's like an Erector set. All the parts are put together according to the plan.

Besides the interior layout, the biggest decision made by the designer is what to use for the space in between the columns. A lot of "modern" construction uses metal studs to build the exterior walls. These studs can be four inches, six inches, or larger in width. Six-inch depth is pretty typical and gives the right depth for insulation. A manufactured panel, typically an exterior-grade gypsum product, goes over the skeleton of the building, and then the finishing treatment (shingles, clapboards, vinyl siding, or even brick) is applied. Exterior treatments have two functions: they determine the look of your building and keep the weather out.

THE WALLS

Once the structural components are completed, and the building is up and dried in, the interior walls are built. The designers might use wood two-by-fours (or two-by-sixes) to fill in the panels. There is actually a lot of benefit to using wood here. Metal doesn't block heat transfer. Wood does. Your insulation goes in between the exterior studs, and with wood this insulation barrier is consistent. Metal studs actually create cold spots. So, if you get a choice, remember wood performs better. (See figure 8.2.)

The choices for the interior structure are pretty much the same as for the exterior: metal or wood and in some cases masonry. The big difference will be that the interior walls will be thinner. With a steel building these interior walls will not be bearing walls, that is, walls that support the weight of the building above them. So if you don't like the size of a room or you want to put in a door, you don't need to worry about anything coming down when you knock a portion of the interior wall out.

THE ROOF STRUCTURE

The structural part of a roof consists of the main carrying members, which can be beams or trusses, and the deck itself. The roofing materials themselves sit on these components. The trusses are those thick zigzag sections you see on the sides of bridges, but smaller. They are deeper than regular beams because that is a more efficient way to carry the weight from above. The deck can be a corrugated metal deck (most common today), wood plank, a manufactured

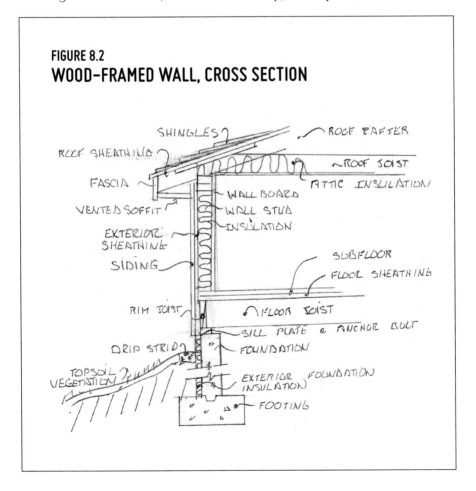

FIGURE 8.2
WOOD-FRAMED WALL, CROSS SECTION

product called Tectum, or even concrete. The roof structure is a whole different animal than the walls and foundation. The length of the supporting members doesn't come into play so much in walls.

The trouble with the roof members, that is, the beams or joists that span the area being covered, is that they can only transfer the load at their ends to the columns or walls that support them; unfortunately, they don't have gravity showing the load the path. They need to use the materials in the member itself; hence, the zigzag sections carry the load along the member to the wall. The force that needs to be transferred is pushing down in the middle of the span, but only being held up at the end. Sometimes this problem is solved by having a very rigid connection where the beam is attached to the supporting member, be it the wall, or another column, at the end. These special connections are expensive and difficult to build, so engineers like to avoid them. It is a lot easier to add another beam going along the length of the roof beam. This cuts the span down and transfers the load to the other walls.

The easiest design to build is one that does not have a flat roof. Put the carrying members at an angle and, at the point where the members meet, a load transfer occurs. Instead of all the weight being carried by the beam to the wall vertically, the load goes along the angle to the wall horizontally. Do this and you'd better take a look at your walls to be sure they don't get knocked over. The walls need to be built to resist the horizontal force. The masonry bond beams discussed previously or beams above the ceiling are designed to accommodate this force.

We don't want to get more deeply into structural engineering, but hopefully this chapter has given a hint of what needs to be considered when you want to change your building.

9 | THE ROOF SYSTEM

THE ROOF SYSTEM is the hardest-working part of your building. You wouldn't think the roof would be too complicated; after all, it just lies around. The chances are you won't even think about your roof until one day you notice a water mark on your ceiling, soft spongy wood on the underside of the roof along a joist, or a piece of your roofing material lying in the parking lot after a storm. Although you won't think about your roof on a daily basis, it will give you more trouble and its upkeep will cost you more than any other component of your structure over the life of the building. The roof literally is the weakest link in the chain, with any or all of the problems below costing a great deal to repair or replace:

- exceeding the life span of the materials
- leaks due to erosion
- improper installation

The main components of the roof are the structure, beams, joists, the deck, the metal deck, wood, Tectum, insulation, and the membrane itself. The details of where the roof connects to the wall are very important. Usually there is some sort of metal flashing that abuts the chimney and other seams to protect the seams from water. The flashing may be copper, a good high-quality choice because it doesn't rust. Aluminum or painted steel is also often used. So as not to be too surprised when the roofing system starts to fail, it's important to know what product is on your building, how old it is, and details about the warranty of your roof. With any luck you will have a record of what has been done. If not, it pays to ask the best roofer in your area to come up and take a look at it. You may find he isn't authorized to make the repairs because it is a competitor's material, but he will tell you if that is the case. He can steer you to the contractor who can do the work.

If you have an old roof that has lots of problems (e.g., leaks, rot), don't waste time or money fixing it. If the roof is at the end of its life cycle or warranty, you should plan on replacing the entire roof; this includes the membrane covering the deck, the shingles, and probably new insulation. You won't really know if you need to do work on the deck and structure until you get the old roof off, but you should plan on some deck and structural replacement anyway. This is especially true if you have visible water damage on your ceilings; because the water has breached the shingles and the membrane, it has probably caused rotting of the deck as well.

It's a really good idea to have an independent inspector observe the work being done on your roof. The independent inspector will identify problems while the work is being completed, thereby guaranteeing that the money you are investing in your new roof solves those problems. The inspector will also help you and the roofing contractor decide when to fix some of the roof structure while the work is under way. It's really important to be able to make decisions quickly when replacing a roof. No contractor can afford to stand around not knowing what to do. The roofer won't wait. He will seal up the roof and wait until a decision is made. This will protect the work that has been done, but it will also cost you twice as much because the contractor will have to return at a later time, remove the new materials (hopefully salvaging what can be saved), make the necessary repairs, and then finish the job. Of course, having the ability to make an informed decision is necessary, but you also need to have enough money in your roof replacement budget to cover not only the expected costs but those unanticipated ones as well.

Remember: *water travels downhill.* If you see water marks on your ceiling, the water probably didn't come from directly above. Chances are good that the leak is far above and the water has worked its way down, soaking the wood, insulation, and plaster, all of which needs to be inspected and repaired or replaced if necessary. This would be an example of an unanticipated expense.

IF YOU NEED A NEW ROOF, WHAT KIND OF DECISIONS DO YOU NEED TO MAKE?

If you have a classic building with slate shingles, try to raise enough money to replace the slate. This stuff is heavy, so your building was built to hold this weight, and slate lasts longer than anything. The roofing industry typically estimates that slate is good for seventy years. The cost premium may be double the cost of other options, but the life span for slate is four times the life span of the other shingle options. If you start seeing spots on the roof where the slate is missing, you will know that it is time to replace your roof. The slate has a tendency to become brittle; it cracks and then falls off. Extreme weather, wind, and ice hasten this process.

If it is not possible to install a slate roof or if you already have asphalt shingles, you still have many choices to make. Asphalt shingles offer many choices of finishes and colors. The manufacturers of shingles also offer a wide range of warranted life spans. A 35-year warranty is quite common, while a 20-year warranty is toward the low end. A great warranty would be upward of 50 years. The high-quality shingle with a long warranty is thicker, the material it is made of will be of higher quality, it will contain more asphalt, and there will be very specific installation instruction details that the roofer will need to follow to justify the longer warranties. These shingles will cost more initially, but the long-term costs will actually be less.

The number of years of the warranty equals the approximate life expectancy of your roof as determined by the manufacturer. The best feature of the warranty is that it enables you to gauge the quality of the product. The longer the warranty, the better the product.

Like all product warranties, roof warranties come with lots of strings attached. The warranty may cover labor and materials (often just materials), and it always contains the blanket statement requiring that "all work be done according to the manufacturer's standard." Oftentimes too, and this is the most valuable aspect, a better-warranted product will limit the contractor who is authorized to install it. The larger shingle manufacturers require that installers be trained in the specifics of the roofing system the manufacturers make and sell. This limits the number of contractors who are authorized to install the product. Even though you had an authorized contractor install your roofing system, any work you have done on your roof since then may still invalidate your warranty. Before you have new mechanical units put on the roof or have a local contractor do some work, check to see how this may affect your warranty. It is the guarantor's job to find loopholes so they don't have to pay out on their warranties!

The warranty issues noted for the shingles apply to the membrane system as well. The membrane is attached to the roof deck, and the shingles are applied on top of it. As with shingles, there are many choices of membranes, and making the decision on which one to use can be very confusing. The membrane can be made of different types of plastic or rubber. These types are called PVC, EDPM, and TPO, with trade names like Sarnafill or Soprema, supplied by companies like Dow Chemical, Firestone, Carlisle, Soprema, and many others. To make the right decisions on which membrane to choose, get a designer to provide specifications that allow all these manufacturers to bid on your roof.

If you have a flat roof, then it consists of a membrane of some sort. In the classic building the membrane might be tar covered by gravel. If it is, consider yourself lucky. Tar and gravel hold up much better than almost anything else. It is self-repairing; when it gets hot, the tar gets soft and fills any cracks that have appeared. You don't see tar and gravel on flat roofs too often for a number of reasons. They are messy, smelly, and time-consuming to put on; and due to the cost of labor and tar, they are expensive. Another major reason you don't see them much anymore is because the roofing industry makes new large membranes and pays distributors to sell them. These membranes come with a decent warranty, are quick to install, and are a great deal cleaner than a tar-and-gravel membrane. Like shingles, these membranes do perform for the life of the warranty. Again, like shingles, the warranty is far shorter than the life of the building. So if you get a chance to create a really long-term maintenance plan, include a couple of brand-new roofs in your budget.

Finally, when deciding on a new roofing system, if you are concerned about your air-conditioning bills, look at the reflectivity of your roofing materials. During the hot days of summer we wear light-colored clothes because they reflect the sunlight and we are much cooler. Unfortunately, if you look at many roofs, they are wearing the equivalent of black T-shirts. Dark colors absorb sunlight, and the resulting heat infiltrates your building. Thus your air-conditioning is running more often to cool the constant supply of hot air, thereby increasing your energy bills. *The more reflective your roofing surface, the lower your cooling bills will be.* For a discussion of the types of roofing products available that qualify for the Energy Star program, check out the Environmental Protection Agency/Department of Energy website for rating information on many types of building materials, including roofing products.[1] When considering the reflectivity of your next roof, remember that the higher the reflectivity number for the product, the cooler your building will be!

NOTE

1. Energy Star, "Reflective Roof Products for Consumers," www.energystar.gov/index.cfm?c=roof_prods.pr_roof_products.

10 | THE WINDOWS

MANY FEEL THAT the most important feature of any building is the windows. How can anyone compare sitting in a windowless room to sitting in one with a big clear expanse of glass looking out onto trees, the sky, or even your neighborhood? The window is where the building and building use meet the rest of the world. The window lets you know what is going on outside, whether it is a gray, wet, miserable day or a gorgeous sunny one. Although windows can be your best friends in the building, unfortunately, they can also be the recalcitrant children of your building. If your predecessors chose poorly or no upgrades have been done to the windows, you may have more of an eyesore and a maintenance headache than with windows of the type you deserve.

In the classic old building the windows were designed big; electric lights were new on the scene and were not expected to provide all the light or the proper quality of light needed. Concerns about energy were different than today's concerns. The focus when your old windows were built was more on the fine woodworking while incorporating the plate glass. The windows had minimal insulation value. Where you might have a decent wall with an insulation value of R-19, your old window with the single pane of glass might have an R of less than R-1. If you have an old building, you most likely have high-quality wood holding a large single pane of glass in a frame constructed with some very clever hardware. If you are in an old building that was remodeled, you may have factory-produced window units that are a standard size fairly close to the windows' original size. These newer units may be wood, wood covered with vinyl (very common), PVC, aluminum, or even fiberglass. They may be operable or fixed, double-hung, casement, awning, arch, or sliders.

If you are in need of new windows, how do you choose? Our modern-day concerns are with the windows' energy usage, cost, and the return on your investment. The price range for different options of greater efficiency varies widely; often the more efficient the window is, the more expensive it becomes.

> **Caveat:** If your building is located in a historic district or if it has been designated as a historic landmark, great care must be taken when dealing with the outward appearance of the building. Before doing any work on the windows, check with your local historical commission. Having the historic landmark designation may add greatly to the cost of replacing or upgrading your windows.

When dealing with window professionals, they will come to you talking about the "R-value" of the various applications they promote. Ask them for the "U-factor" information based on the National Fenestration Rating Council's (NFRC's) ratings parameters. (The term *fenestration* refers to any opening in a building's envelope, including windows, doors, and skylights.)[1] If your window expert doesn't know what the NFRC rating system is and is using the R-value and not talking about the U-factor, then the chances are good that he is selling you an inferior product with decreased energy efficiency (but at a premium price). The NFRC takes the entire window into account, not just the glass. According to the NFRC, the U-factor takes into consideration how the windows are affected not only by solar radiation but also by the air that flows around them. The U-factor measures the actual heat that is lost by the window, while the R-value measures how resistant the window is to heat loss. The U-factor deals with the emissivity of the glass, or the ability of the glass to absorb and radiate the energy through itself and out of or into the room. During the last ten years significant product development has resulted in the evolution of low-e (low emissivity) coatings. These windows far outperform windows made using earlier technologies, and as they become more readily available, the price for these items decreases. A high-quality window should have a low U-factor and a high R-value. (See figure 10.1.) Additional ratings for a high-quality window include a low *solar heat gain coefficient* (how well a product blocks heat from the sun), a low *air leakage* rating (the amount of air that passes through cracks in the window assembly), a high *condensation resistance* rating (the product's ability to resist the formation of condensation on its interior), and consideration of the *visible transmittance*, or how much light comes through the window. The higher the visible transmittance rating, the more light that comes through that can damage your interior materials.[2] (See figure 10.2.)

Several years ago, the preferred option for upgrading windows was to add what was referred to then as a storm window, instead of replacing the actual

FIGURE 10.1
R-VALUES OF WINDOWS

Single Glass	**0.91**
with storm	2.00
Double insulating glass	
3/16" air space	1.61
1/4" air space	1.69
1/2" air space	2.04
3/4" air space	2.38
1/2" with low-E 0.20	3.13
with suspended film	2.77
with two suspended films	3.85
with suspended film and low-E	4.05
Triple insulating glass	
1/4" air spaces	2.56
1/2" air spaces	3.23
Addition for tight-fitting drapes or shades, or closed blinds	**0.29**

window. Units like this are no longer considered a viable solution. With all the improvements in window construction and the employment of new technology, it is felt that the better solution for increased energy efficiency is window replacement.

When looking at new windows you will be presented with various types of construction options. Your new windows should have at least two panes, but three panes of glass are not uncommon. The gap between the panes will contain a vacuum or be filled with dry regular air or an inert gas. When purchasing new windows, you must take into consideration not only the glass but the frame, operability, and color as well. The different window options come with various advantages as well as costs. Window frames made of wood will give you good energy performance affordably. Windows constructed with fiberglass frames are more expensive, but it is claimed that they offer greater

FIGURE 10.2
NATIONAL FENESTRATION RATING COUNCIL LABEL

World's Best Window Co.
Millennium 2000+
Vinyl-Clad Wood Frame
Double Glazing • Argon Fill • Low E
Product Type: **Vertical Slider**

ENERGY PERFORMANCE RATINGS

U-Factor (U.S./I-P)	Solar Heat Gain Coefficient
0.35	**0.32**

ADDITIONAL PERFORMANCE RATINGS

Visible Transmittance	Air Leakage (U.S./I-P)
0.51	**0.2**

Condensation Resistance	
51	**—**

energy efficiency because the fiberglass frames are glass. The sales representative will tell you that the frame is glass, just like the windowpane, so the pane and the frame expand and contract at the same rate and this keeps the unit tight (i.e., more energy efficient). These and other material candidates utilize flexible glazing compounds that may make this a moot point. The fiberglass will hold up well over time but isn't necessarily more energy efficient. The next windows on the price scale are those that are made of vinyl frames. These windows offer good quality at an affordable price.

If you have large windows, then your window professional will use the term *storefront*. Instead of having a manufactured window unit, a metal frame is installed in the opening, and then the glass is placed within the frame. Think of it as a window wall. These windows can and do perform very well from an energy standpoint. Even though the frame is aluminum, there is a gasket between the inner and outer frame pieces. It acts as a thermal brake. The glass units themselves have all the variety available in the industry as far as how many panes of glass there are, how thick the gap between them is, and how thick each pane of glass is. These are the way to go with big openings. Aluminum window units are built with aluminum frames in sizes on a par with the previously mentioned wood and vinyl ones. These windows perform well, are cost-effective, and are very popular with institutional installations because they offer low maintenance and long-term operability. The cost of these units would, however, be more expensive than standard-sized windows.

Two other major considerations when choosing new windows are operability and color. Operability can be a painful choice. If you are choosing windows for offices or classrooms, you need to decide if you should let the users open the windows or not. The windows' interaction with the heat management system in your building must be a major consideration when making this decision. If your windows open, the heat management system must be able to compensate for this. If your heating system senses that the room is too cold or hot, it will correct the temperature by running the system. The room next door may not have a thermostat, so the comfort of that room is compromised—too hot or too cold. If you choose operability, learn how the temperature control system works and be sure to manage it. Maintenance is anther big issue with operability. Most of your leaky building issues might just be because the windows were left open. Security is an issue too, but if a decent lock doesn't solve security issues, there is more that needs to be done than fix the windows.

Color and the associated issue of reflectance are the most important aesthetic considerations. Reflectance will relate to your heat gain and R-values.

As you are walking through your building, do you notice that the once beautiful tapestry rug in your reading room is faded when you move the chair next to the window? As you moved the chair, did you notice that the chair didn't look as lush and subtle, so you turn the cushion over and see that it is a different color on the unexposed side? The bleaching effect of sun on interior materials may actually be why you decide to go with a high-value window upgrade. The more reflectance you choose, the darker your building will be. Remember, the south-facing units will experience the greatest heat gain, the north will have the greatest loss, and the east will give you warm mornings, the west warm afternoons. A good designer will provide recommendations on where and how you choose the reflectance of your new windows.

Caveat: When you are removing old windows, beware because the old ones may contain lead-based paint. You need to make sure you formally notify the contractor of the status of the windows and require the contractor to show their licensing, insurance, and training to manage lead-based paint removal. As long as the contractor is qualified and has been formally notified, they will have the ability and training to handle this problem properly.

If you can't afford new windows, there are ways to inexpensively increase the efficiency of the current windows. The key to energy efficiency is to achieve a balance between heat gain and loss by convection and conduction in order to create a setting where people can comfortably interact. If your building is not insulated, you have very large, old windows, and there are lots of granite or marble flooring and counters, your challenge is great. The presence of these three things creates a considerable impediment to comfort because the heat of our bodies is not sufficient to overcome the cold of the building. In the summer, the sunlight comes in through our windows, superheating the air and thus reducing the efficacy of our air conditioners. So even though our thermostats are reading what should be comfortable temperatures, our bodies perceive the temperatures very differently. Our goal is to try to manipulate what we perceive the temperature to be through a few simple exercises:

1. Allow the sun to penetrate south windows when it is present in the winter; otherwise use blinds and shades.

2. Help the building's heating system to warm the interior by install-ing better thermal insulation in the walls and ceilings and multiple layers of glass and/or insulating curtains. *Good thermal insulation of a building pays off in increased radiant comfort.*

3. Use highly reflective surfaces to reflect body heat back to the body.

4. Open a building to the night air, allowing warm surfaces to radiate their heat into space.

Windows are one of the largest sources of heat and air loss that force the heating or air-conditioning unit to work harder. Remember our lesson on the thermodynamic principles of conduction, convection, and infrared heating. A pane of glass will conduct (*lose*) interior heat through the pane to the *cold* outside air. Conduction occurs due to heated air particles naturally seeking to move to lower energy states (cold = less energetic air). When heat is lost by conduction from the air next to windows, the cooled air then sinks and pulls more warm air against the window. This process, called convection, establishes a continual current that will cool your home throughout the night. Infrared is heat from the sun that comes from light shining through your windows and warming your home. Even on a cloudy day, letting light shine through your windows will collect solar heat energy inside your building.

During the summer months, east or west windows generate the most solar heat gain. During the summer, if shade trees do not exist around your building, then hood awnings, Venetian awnings, or exterior roll blinds would be the best option for keeping direct sunlight out. If none of these options is possible, then an interior shading system is better than nothing. These systems include cellular blinds, window quilts, and window film. During the winter months, those same east- and west-facing windows are responsible for heat loss. In the winter, south-facing windows provide for some solar heat gain during the day as long as the windows are in proper working order (caulked and tightly closed), so a window treatment should be opened on sunny winter days and closed on cloudy winter days and always at night.

POSSIBLE SOLUTIONS
CELLULAR WINDOW BLINDS

The U.S. Department of Energy reported that window treatments such as cellular blinds can reduce energy waste/cost by 20 percent.[3] (See figure 10.3.) Not all window coverings reduce energy waste/cost. Window quilts are the most energy-efficient coverings, but they have functional style limitations.

Bamboo blinds, wood blinds, and mini-blinds offer varying degrees of insulation, but without some kind of additional liner their insulating value is minimal. Cellular shades when combined with an energy-efficient sidetrack (used to keep the blinds in place) are reported to offer five times the thermal performance even on the most energy-inefficient windows.

WINDOW QUILTS

Materials can be purchased to make custom window quilts. The window quilt itself comprises four layers to maximize the benefit of the quilt.[4] These layers are

1. a warm, dry, moisture-resistant lining

2. high-density needled hollow fibers

3. a reflective polyethylene vapor barrier

4. metallized Mylar with needled, air-trapping polyester fibers

For maximum efficiency, the window quilt system must have three components: insulating fabric as described above, a decorative fabric cover, and a

FIGURE 10.3
CELLULAR BLIND

magnetic edge seal. Just as with cellular blinds, the maximum benefit of a window quilt system is realized when a magnetic edge seal is used. This seal creates an airtight barrier to keep heat in during the winter and out during the summer.[5]

WINDOW FILMS

Window films can be applied to all windows for decreased solar heat gain. Because 40 percent of unwanted heat comes through your windows, the use of reflective window coatings redirects that heat before it comes into your building. Reflective window coatings are large sheets of plastic that are treated with dyes or thin layers of metal. A secondary benefit is that the window film will reduce sun damage and glare. Large-scale utilization of window film can have a dramatic impact on your energy usage, especially in warm climates.[6] The manufacturers of window film are continually improving the product and how it is used. Look for professional installers in your area to highlight the different options available and help you decide what would be the best application for your purposes.

Caveat: With the window film option you would still have to purchase window covers for all the windows in order to keep the heat from exiting during the winter months; window films are basically a warm weather solution.

NOTES
1. National Fenestration Rating Council, www.nfrc.org/documents/U-Factor.pdf.
2. Adapted with permission from the National Fenestration Rating Council.
3. Cellularwindowshades.com, "Proven Savings on Cooling and Heating Costs," http://cellularwindowshades.com/energysmart.html.
4. Lisa Murgatroyd, "Thermal Curtains: Making Your Windows Warm," www.humboldt.edu/~ccat/virtualtour/handouts/thermal_curtains.pdf.
5. The Warm Company, "Shades for Comfort: What Do Window Treatments Have to Do with Saving Energy? Warm Window Insulated Shade System," www.warmcompany.com/warmwindow/Warm.pdf.
6. FacilitiesNet, "Window Film Saves Energy at Stanford University," www.facilitiesnet.com/casestudies/details.asp?GeneralID=17054.

<table>
<tr><td>11</td><td></td></tr>
</table>

11 | INTERIOR FINISHES

NOW THAT YOU have an understanding of how your structure was built, the focus will turn to how it was finished. Once the foundation, walls, roof, siding, and utilities are complete, the next phase of the construction involves a major shift in the process. The foremen, builders, and laborers embark on a phase experts call "getting dried in." They turn their attention to the interior of the building, making the shell not only habitable but ready for interior decorating.

If you are in an old building or have lived in an old house, you may have noticed, while doing any project that involves cutting into the walls, thin pieces of wood that run horizontally across the studs or chicken wire attached to the studs. Before the sealing coat could be applied to the walls, the builders had to install this lath or wire so the plaster mud would have something to adhere to. Then they would trowel on a mixture of plaster mud to a smooth surface. Once that was dry, the finish coats were applied.

This method provided many old buildings with high-quality, long-lasting walls. As long as it isn't saturated with moisture, the wall can be cleaned. If it is damaged by impact or moisture, it can be repaired. Although new gypsum compounds can be used, it is best to bring in an experienced tradesperson who will determine what the original compound was made of, mix up a batch of plaster that mimics the original material, and then apply a finish. You have found a great tradesperson if you can't tell the repaired wall space from the original. To see an experienced tradesperson do this is to witness an artist at work.

THE DRYWALL

If you aren't putting up plaster walls, then the next and really only option is the installation of drywall, also known as Sheetrock or gypsum board. No matter what the finish on the wall is going to be, the project is at the stage where the inside of the building is covered. From the most basic home or apartment to the most expensive, fully detailed mansion or office space, the wall comprises drywall screwed to the studs. The drywall itself is a product of gypsum plaster (a soft white or gray mineral consisting of hydrated calcium sulfate) that is pressed between two sheets of thick paper and then kiln dried. Drywall is the canvas on which future work (i.e., painting, wallpapering, or paneling) is done. It has the added benefit of insulating, with R-values from .32 for ⅜-inch board to .83 for 1-inch board. Not only does it provide an insulating quality, but it also helps reduce sound transmission between rooms.

Drywall is drywall is drywall. The only variation is in the thickness, the moisture resistance, and the size. The material that it is made of doesn't change. Drywall comes in various thicknesses, the most common being ⅝ inch or ½ inch. The contractor also has a choice on the size of the board. He will choose the size that gives him the fewest joints to finish, or "tape," in the parlance of the trade. The standard size is 4 feet by 8 feet, with ⅜-inch thickness. He might use 4 feet by 10 feet or 12 feet on the ceilings. Some drywall is rated as fire resistant. It has a special designation on its label of either "Type X" or "Type C." Regular building drywall has a fire resistance of thirty minutes, while Type X has been rated to provide one hour of fire protection and Type C provides even greater protection.[1] This fire-resistant drywall is made by adding glass fibers to the gypsum mud before it is pressed and kiln dried. Fire-resistant drywall is commonly used when two distinct parts of your building touch (such as your garage and your house) or in utility closets with boilers or hot water tanks. You should check your local building codes to see what if any special regulations concerning fire protection must be adhered to.

Other materials used in the drywall installation include J strips, corner beads, tape, and the joint compound (mud). The corner bead will be used to add strength and structural integrity to the corners. It is made of either metal or plastic, is placed over the drywall, and ideally is screwed into place. It runs the length of the drywall sheet, or from floor to ceiling if you are seaming boards. Taping compound covers the bead and is smoothed over with mud when the joints are being done. A J strip is installed to finish the board against a window. Properly installed drywall abuts the window, so the J strip is placed to create a finished look. The J strip is usually plastic. It doesn't require any finish and often won't take paint, so a neutral color needs to be chosen. White is usually safe. The finish against doors usually isn't an issue because the rough-cut corner is covered by the frame or by the trim.

The boards should be put up vertically, with the longest dimension going up and down along the studs. The boards are then attached to the studs with countersunk drywall screws. These are placed 8 to 12 inches apart on the perimeter and 16 inches apart in the field of the board. Remember, every screw must be covered with mud and sanded, repeatedly, so don't go crazy with the drywall screws. The most prevalent tool you will see in use is the electric screw gun, and with an experienced installer, the process is something to watch. Once the process starts and the boards are in place, the screw guns rarely shut off. They run constantly, slapping screws in every few seconds. The installers know when the screw is in by the sound. There is the buzz of the screw gun, then a *crank* when the screw is in, and then on to the next board. The tricky part comes when dealing with the electric outlet boxes in the wall or the junction boxes for the lights. The installers measure the location, measure and trace the shape of the box on the drywall, and then use a keyhole saw to cut out the boxes. There isn't much room for error when making these cuts. If the installer measures and the cut is even only a little off, it is a flaw always to be seen.

When all the drywall is up, then the tapers come in. These are the tradespeople who cover up the joints and get the board ready for the real finish. An expert crew will fill all the joints in three separate coats. The first step is to apply a generous amount of joint compound or "mud." Then a paper strip called the tape is applied and smoothed out with the "knife" (i.e., a putty knife—much like a spatula). The size of the knife depends on which coat of mud is being applied. The knives start thin, about 3 inches across, and get wider at the finish, maybe 8 inches across. Make sure that the knife is smooth, in order to limit the amount of sanding, and clean, so that rust doesn't taint the mud and bleed through the paint. The environment in the building becomes very important at this stage of the project. The taping process puts a lot of water into the air. Before the tapers can go on to the next step in the process, the mud has to cure dry. If it is cold and wet outside, make sure all the windows are closed, because the added humidity will impede the drying process. If it is not cold or raining, opening the windows and using fans to move dry air around the room will expedite the curing process.

Once the taping is complete the sanders come in. This step requires skill, and, if it is not done correctly, it will make extra work for the tapers and may forever be reflected in your finish. If there is good talent on the taping side, one can get away with sanding after the third coat. It is more prudent to sand after the second coat, and again after the third. After the third coat the work is expected to be ready for the finish, usually paint.

If you have rooms that require a special finish, say a quiet room with acoustic paneling, you still need to drywall, but then only one coat of taping is required. The paneling system would go on over the drywall, so there is no need for a high-grade finish. This saves you money on the finish end, because you don't need a paint-grade finish.

HOW DO THE FINISHES GET CHOSEN?

The number of choices for the finished look is endless, depending on availability, cost, and how much time you have. Although this rarely happens with commercial projects, it is a good idea to press for decisions on the type of finish that will be implemented very early on in the design process. The designer should present you with a color board for your review, comments, and approval. This board will include the color or type of wall finish, examples of the types of flooring material and color, the window color, base color, door and door frame color, and maybe even ceiling considerations too. Some of these products may require special orders, manufacturing, and production, so get this process under way as soon as possible so your project deadlines aren't missed because the wallpaper your team selected isn't readily available. If you are working with a designer, don't be afraid to let her do her work. If you micromanage things, the coordination might not work as well.

PAINT

Once you decide that your finish is going to be paint, there are a few things to keep in mind. Never use cheap or damaged paint. Try doing a ceiling with cheap paint just once and you will never buy cheap paint again. There will be more on you and the floor than on the ceiling. Aside from the quality of the paint, the secret to a good paint job lies in the preparation that goes into the project. Ideally, the primer coat should be applied before the drywall crew leaves and the wall is inspected with them. Once the primer is on the wall, areas that need more sanding will be obvious, and the drywall crew should take care of that. Bring a bright light to inspect the wall after the primary coat is dry. Use a pencil to mark areas that need more sanding. Never use a pen; it will bleed through any finish you put on and will lead to one of those dreaded flaws. Don't underestimate the time it takes to do the job right. Don't skimp and don't let the contractor skimp.

STEPS TO A SUCCESSFUL PAINT JOB

1. Vacate the area.

2. Insist on tarps on the floor, even an unfinished one.

3. Mask off what you don't want painted or splattered with paint.

4. Provide ventilation; this helps cure the paint.

5. Use the right tools:
   a. brushes and rollers designated for the type of paint finish you are using
   b. proper ladders and scaffolding as needed

6. Prepping. If it is a new wall, the painter will want to sand first, even if the drywaller has done this. A high-quality painter is proud of the finish he achieves, so if he insists on a day or two of sanding, let him do it. You don't want a patch or touch-up showing on a finished wall. If you do, it will always look like a patch.

7. If you don't trust the painter, insist that he wait for your approval before moving on to the next coat.

8. Insist on at least two finish coats.

The choices you will be asked to make include the color and the finish of the paint. The finish is how the paint will look after it cures. If you go to any good hardware or paint store, they will have paint chips that allow you to compare the various finishes. You will be asked to choose between smooth and soft, satin or eggshell. In high-abuse areas consider using epoxy. Although it may be twice the price, it will hold up to the cleaning, dirt, and traffic that come with the territory of a bathroom or kitchen area. When it comes to the application process, there are a number of choices there as well. One system uses spray guns to apply the paint to the surface, while the preferred method for a consistent high-quality finish is the roller method.

WOOD FINISH

It would be really nice if there were a room or two fancy enough for the finish to be wood, or millwork. That is the fancy name for cabinetry. There is no need for drywall on these walls. The wood is applied directly to the studs, just like the drywall. The choices here are many. You could install 4-by-8-foot sheets of paneling, just like the styles of the 1960s. This type of paneling consists of a laminated sheet of very thin plywood. It is really wood and is prefinished, so you save money because you don't have to hire a drywaller, taper, or painter. The carpentry skills needed for the work are not high either. For a truly sophisticated look of the highest design quality, true wood paneling is the way to go. The architect draws the plan for the woodwork and submits that to the builder, who then finds a mill to provide the wood for the panels to specification. True boards of ¾ inch (real finished thickness) by 6, 8, 10, or 12 inches or even greater width are milled, and depending on the project, custom lathe work may be required to create special routed edges on the boards, which are put together and topped off for a high-quality finish.

WALLPAPER FINISH

If your building, or desire, rests in between paint and wood, wallpaper may be what you want. The finish for wallpaper on the drywall is the same as paint. The wallboard has to be totally smooth for a high-quality wallpaper job. The choices for wallpaper are endless, of course, and vary in their texture, material, pattern, and color. Being distinctive and a visionary would be great assets in choosing wallpaper. Always hire the most experienced professional you can find, because wallpapering is a complicated process, and wallpaper can easily look bad if it has not been properly seamed and pasted.

FLOORING

Nothing sets the tone for the space more than the floor. It is the base for everything else you can see. The variety of effects you can get from carpet or vinyl floor patterns is infinite. The choice can reflect modern, traditional, ethnic, expensive, economical, or utilitarian views. Choosing the floor is a critical step in the design process and shouldn't be taken lightly.

When you create a new space or renovate an existing one, your choice of floor will be carpet, vinyl, or wood. Depending on the quality of the product, a good rule of thumb is that vinyl flooring will be the least expensive option to install, while wood is the most expensive item to install; over the long term, however, the vinyl will cost more because it will have to be replaced, whereas wood may only have to be refinished but not replaced. The maintenance cost of vinyl is also more than that of carpeting. Although the vinyl floor will hold up under heavy, abusive traffic, it doesn't offer the same advantages as carpet. Carpeting is quiet. It feels better to walk on. It sends a psychological message that the space is finished and should be respected.

Many of us have old carpeting in our buildings. It is probably made of wool or other natural fibers and can withstand a lot of wear and tear. If it is maintained properly—by regular, methodical use of a high-quality vacuum cleaner—it can last for decades. Ideally, if you are replacing carpeting, putting down a rug of a natural fiber such as wool should be your first choice. Wool carpet retains its resilience and new appearance longer than conventional synthetic carpets because of its inherent properties, which allow the fibers to bounce back after the carpet is walked on or a piece of furniture is moved. This unique quality makes wool carpet a special value when considering longevity of carpet. Wool carpeting is flame resistant because of the moisture contained in the fibers. It is also nontoxic, nonallergenic, and deters bacterial growth. The moisture content of wool also reduces static electricity (important around your computers). Wool carpet purifies the indoor air of common contaminants like formaldehyde, nitrogen dioxide, and sulfur dioxide by locking the contaminants deep in the core of the fibers. Wool carpets' natural fibers form millions of tiny air pockets that regulate the temperature; the air pockets act as insulation and thus help reduce energy bills.[2] Natural-fiber carpet is going to cost more to install, but you will only have to replace it once every 50 to 60 years. This differs from many of the new carpet materials, which are petroleum-based by-products and only have a life span of approximately 10 years, so plan on all of the expense and on adding carpeting to the landfill every decade! Remember, when figuring out the cost of a carpet, you should include the ancillary expenses of the installation such as boxing and moving your collections, storing your collections, moving and reassembling shelves, and the number of days you must close off your facility in order to complete the project. Whatever carpeting you decide on, when you replace the carpet, take advantage of the offer of free training from the manufacturer to learn how to clean it. Proper maintenance of the material will help prolong the life of the rug. If you do your own cleaning, spend some money and buy a high-quality industrial vacuum cleaner to help prolong the life of your carpet.

Whether you are installing carpet or vinyl, the base you are putting the product on has to be smooth and well cured. If you are putting carpeting down on a new concrete floor, never rush the project. The new products want the moisture levels to be very low prior to installation. Because concrete is full of water when it is made, it can take a very long time for the moisture to leave the floor. If you put a carpet on "wet" concrete, you may experience mold problems, rippling, and an accelerated degradation and disintegration of the carpet or vinyl. If you are placing a carpet on a new floor, make sure the installer uses a cement or acrylic-based patching compound to smooth it out. This isn't an expensive step and should be done automatically by a qualified carpet installer.

BUT YOU REALLY LIKE WOOD

Wood flooring comes in a variety of options. You can choose anything from less expensive, micro-thin, prefinished composite flooring to very expensive floors made of milled hardwood. Other choices include the new cork floors and many other new wood flooring options with a wide range of quality and prices. After cost, the main consideration when selecting a wood floor is the wear the floor will get. A high-quality wood floor is constructed of thick (¾-inch) hardwood for a reason. These floors can be sanded and refinished often, while the less expensive materials are actually veneer and scratch easily. Although these veneer floors may seem to be the most affordable option, they cannot be sanded or refinished, so a scratch is there forever. The newest innovation on the market is cork flooring. It is soft and very porous. Be sure you understand how to protect it before you decide on it. It is a very user-friendly floor designed for wet use. It is new, though, so the jury may still be deliberating on its long-term viability in public applications.

CONCRETE FLOORS

Every building has some concrete floors. It is a good idea to have these sealed in some way. Concrete is porous, and a sealer will keep the stains and moisture out to some degree. The concrete floor also acts as a moisture sink during warm weather. The moisture in there will condense upon the cooler floor and is stored there. The environment you can maintain will be better if you seal the floor. A clear sealer is an option, but a colored coating does add some value. It can be lighter in tone than the concrete, making visibility better and providing a much cleaner look. A little abrasive finish makes it safer as well.

Concrete floors can get fancy too. In new installations one can find stamped and colored concrete. When this process is done properly, the resulting floor will look like tile. The look could be similar to old classic tile flooring, or it could be a custom collage of colors and designs. It is designed for areas of high abuse, like lobbies or even restrooms. This can add a nice touch to an area.

TERRAZZO FLOOR

If you have an old building with a beautiful, multicolored chip floor, then you may have a terrazzo floor. A terrazzo floor is the same as any concrete slab, with a few exceptions. Popular during construction in the late nineteenth and early twentieth centuries, this flooring may actually have been discovered accidentally during the fifteenth century. Mosaic artists had the habit of sweeping the waste marble chips out the door onto their terraces. After walking over them they found that the surface smoothed out, so they started putting the chips into clay and then polished the surface with heavy stones for a permanent flooring material. Examples of terrazzo floors include St. Peter's Basilica and George Washington's Mount Vernon home.[3]

A terrazzo floor is basically a specialized concrete slab that is put down in a layer from ½- to ¾-inch thick. Once the concrete is down, colored marble chips are dispersed on the surface while the mix is fresh. The chips are then set in during the floating or trawling process. After the mixture hardens, the polishing process begins. Large floor-grinding machines using diamond chip-impregnated cutters polish the surface in steps from rough to fine.

CERAMIC OR QUARRY TILE

Ceramic and quarry tiles are designed for high-abuse public spaces. Floors made of ceramic or quarry tile are hard; they don't stain and will stand up to cleaners. They are expensive but are available in a great variety of colors and sizes. They provide a high-quality finish, especially if accent tiles and patterns are used.

THE CEILING

Tin ceilings were very popular in the late nineteenth and early twentieth centuries. Originally designed to allow people the beauty of a sculptured plaster ceiling or ornamental stucco decoration without the high cost, they graced Victorian homes and stores in many areas of the United States. The cost of sculptured plaster ceilings was out of reach for many builders at that time, so the alternative was to use a stamped tin plate to simulate the elegance and beauty of a sculptured ceiling. The tin ceiling tiles were also used to cover over unsightly plastered or damaged ceilings. Tin ceilings had an added benefit—they were a good fire barrier. Many stores had apartments over them, and if a store caught fire, the occupants of the upstairs apartment had a much greater chance of survival due to the fire barrier resistance of the tin ceiling plates.

Over a period of many years, tin ceilings were replaced with ceiling tile, and the beautiful arrangements of tin ceiling tiles were generally covered over with everything from wallboard and plaster to suspended ceilings. So acoustic ceilings in older buildings aren't always quite what they seem.

Acoustic ceilings are inexpensive, relatively easy to install, and do provide the best access to your heating and lighting ducts, pipes, conduits, and junction boxes. In modern construction, if you don't have acoustic ceilings, you have a building designed in a different, probably more expensive way. There will be plenums above the ceiling and chases throughout the building to accommodate the mechanicals. You probably have water-based heating systems as well. And no room for air ducts.

What are acoustic ceilings made of anyway? They can be considered a good "green" material, because their tiles are primarily made of recycled paper. A large painted grid that is made of either steel or aluminum is attached to the existing ceiling. The system hangs by wires from the structure above, which includes the floor joists. That means if you have a lightweight design and there is bouncing upstairs, your ceiling will be moving. The ceiling also supports your lights. There should be extra wires at the lights, so they can't fall out if the grid moves. The pipes, ductwork, and sprinklers all should be supported by the structure. New codes require seismic constraints to be used to contain all the things above the suspended ceiling during a seismic event.

Acoustic ceiling tiles do discolor after a while, mostly due to particles in the air, or to the lighting, sunlight, or ultraviolet rays (the bane of exposed materials), but these ceiling systems can last for a long time. When the tiles all discolor together, it doesn't look wrong. The most common problem will be around the heat grilles in the ceiling. The air being blown either in or out the ducts carries dust and leaves a mess on the grille. It's hard to clean, and even a good system will leave residue over time.

To clean your suspended ceiling system, a vacuum cleaner might do a good job. If it's grease from the air duct you are trying to get off, you will probably have only limited success. The easiest way to maintain a fresh-looking suspended ceiling system, and this is done a lot, is to mix a little paint to the same color tone as the ceiling, brush it on, and don't tell anyone.

So you are thinking of installing a new suspended ceiling. The possibilities are quite varied. The lowest-cost alternative for purchase and installation is a 2-by-4-foot white acoustic tile system. Remember that all these tiles have an acoustic suppression quality, but they vary in degrees of sound attenuation. The product material lists an STC rating (sound transmission coefficient). They are available in varying degrees of quietness. A new ceiling of 2-by-2-foot acoustic tiles costs significantly more because you need more grids, ceiling tiles, and a lot more labor. A good compromise between the two is a product that looks like 2 by 2 feet but is actually 2 by 4 feet. Only the discriminating eye can see where there is tile but no grid. It's a good value.

To really add some pop to a ceiling renovation, consider incorporating different levels of height. You can separate different sections in a large room with a low section and a higher section in the middle. This is expensive—there is a lot of framing, drywall, and paint—but it adds a whole new level to the design. Lighting and color complete the effect. This is one place where a generous budget will make a big difference to the final product.

NOTES

1. Drywall How To Manual, www.drywallhowto.com/fire-resistant.shtml.
2. About.com, "Interior Decorating," http://interiordec.about.com/gi/dynamic/ offsite.htm?zi=1/XJ/Ya&sdn=interiordec&cdn=homegarden&tm=11&gps=75_ 696_1004_637&f=00&tt=14&bt=0&bts=0&st=31&zu=http%3A//www.parish -supply.com/wool.htm.
3. This Old House, www.thisoldhouse.com/toh/photos/0,,20055568,00.html.

<table>
<tr><td>12</td><td>

THE PLAN IT/DO IT PROFESSIONALS

</td></tr>
</table>

ONCE YOU HAVE looked at your building critically, the next step is to find professionals you can trust to help you achieve your project goals. In this chapter we will examine the different types of professionals, credentials and certifications, billing practices, how to request and evaluate proposals, and how to make certain that the work is done up to code and the specifications of the proposal. In cases where you have a specific problem such as lighting, plumbing, or heating, it is best to contact a specific service professional to deal with the issue. If you have a problem that involves the coordination of several different service professionals, then it is best to contact a contractor or architect who can coordinate the project with those professionals. You will want a team leader who manages the process so things are done in the correct order and who keeps the process on task as well as on budget. (A chart showing the phases of a typical building renovation project is shown in figure 12.1.)

ARCHITECT

What is an architect anyway? Many people can trace their understanding of architects to the book by the writer Ayn Rand titled *The Fountainhead.* This book (and the movie based on it) created a perception of architects that was both a blessing and a curse to the architectural community. One thing it did

FIGURE 12.1
LIBRARY BASEMENT RENOVATION

ID	⊙	Task Name	Resource Names	Duration	Predecessors	Start	Finish
1	▥	**Basement Renovations**	Owner	0 days		Tue 1/12/10	Tue 1/12/10
2		**Preliminary Phase**		**24 days**		**Mon 1/4/10**	**Tue 4/13/10**
3	▥	Identify committee	Owner	1 day		Mon 1/4/10	Wed 1/6/10
4	▥	Committee Vote to Move forward	Owner	0 days		Tue 1/12/10	Tue 1/12/10
5		Identify designer	Owner	1 day	3	Thu 1/7/10	Mon 1/11/10
6		Conceptual design complete	Designer	5 days	3	Thu 1/7/10	Wed 1/27/10
7		Perform cost estimate	Designer	3 days	6	Thu 1/28/10	Tue 2/9/10
8		Complete final design	Designer	15 days	7	Wed 2/10/10	Tue 4/13/10
9	▥	**Acquire funding**	Owner	0 days	8	Tue 4/13/10	Tue 4/13/10
10		**Construction Phase**		**54 days**	**9**	**Wed 4/14/10**	**Thu 11/25/10**
11		**Rough in Phase**		**34 days**		**Wed 4/14/10**	**Thu 9/2/10**

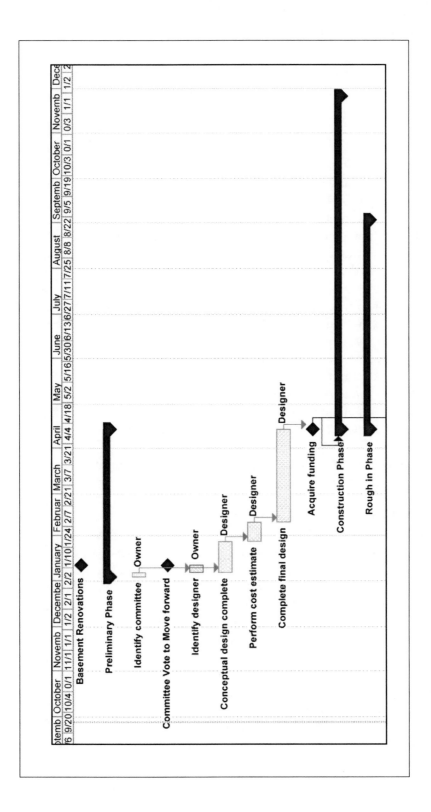

was to help establish the architect as a dominant force in the working of the world. It encouraged the idea that mankind's ambitions, possibilities, and weaknesses could be incorporated into the design and building process. The downside of the book is that it illuminated the architect's ego. Interactions with some architects leave us wondering why we would ever want to work with these professionals, given their large egos. It's not right to paint the entire profession with this brush, though. When you find a good architect that you can build rapport with and work with, you will appreciate his experience and benefit from his vast knowledge base.

Becoming an architect involves an advanced education and an exacting training. At a minimum, an architect has a baccalaureate degree and very likely a master's degree. Many practicing architects have taken the extra steps to become a "registered architect." After apprenticing or working under a competent professional for a time, the architect sits for a nationally recognized exam. The exam is administered over the course of several days and has various components, depending on the state in which the exam is given. The topics covered on the exam include all components of the building process that the architect is responsible for. It is prudent to remember when looking at a nice new modern building that this only represents the most visible and dramatic results of the architectural effort expended. An enormous amount of work and knowledge have gone into designing that building.

The typical architect must have a working knowledge of topics such as occupant count, egress distance, fire ratings, materials, air movement, and light, as well as the basics of structural design, site layout, bearing capacity, and mechanical, electrical, and fire protection systems. He is also responsible for knowing about accessibility (handicapped) requirements, state laws, federal laws, and local building and life safety codes. All of these things must be taken into consideration before the architect even sits down to draw up your aesthetically pleasing plan. Your architect will agree to provide all of his expertise in one package, and he should also coordinate and supervise your construction project. Depending on the size of your project, figure on spending in the neighborhood of 5 to 15 percent of your total budget on architectural services. Because it takes an architect many smaller projects to achieve his annual earning goals, you should expect to pay a higher percentage of your total budget for architectural services on a smaller project than on a large one. The magnitude of the project may be smaller, but the amount of work is the same as that of a larger project. Remember, when you hire the architect, unless it's a small firm, you will also have hired his staff. The staff includes the CADD (computer-aided design and drafting) drafters, a job captain (the principal doesn't usually do the detail work), the subconsultants, and office staff. The subconsultants will be the designers for any work you need beyond the pure architectural considerations. If there are building structure concerns, a structural engineering firm will be retained. The same holds true for mechanical, electrical, site, acoustic, or other special needs. Interior designers will help with the finishes. These are often part of the in-house staff. You are paying for access to all of this expertise, and you will be billed on a monthly basis for these services once you retain (sign contracts) your architectural firm. (For a chart of the various professionals involved in a building project, see figure 12.2.)

PICKING THE ARCHITECT

The architectural firm will have been chosen by you, based on your project criteria and committee requirements. To initiate the process, you send out a request for proposal (RFP) to the design community. To find architects, contact your local branch of the American Institute of Architects (AIA).[1] Contact those firms that have experience and/or styles that reflect the requirements of your committee. Invite them to respond to your RFP. Firms that are interested will then send you a letter and probably a nice glossy brochure. From those respondents, you and your committee will select those firms you wish to interview. At this point the firm will come in and listen to the goals, dreams, aspirations, and limitations of the committee. This is often the most instructive part of the design process. It is where the real dialogue and thoughts are shared, the most exciting step in the total process. Everyone is excited, engaged, and very anxious to start work.

Enough can't be said about having a committee working together at this stage of the building process. Appointing a committee to make critical decisions, such as the firm to be hired, helps create ownership and pride in the project. If you can get everyone on board with a joint decision, you will have a much more successful building program. Having a committee will reduce any second-guessing and foster more support for the project during both the good times and the rough ones. It is recommended that you have a recording secretary keep track of all meetings. It is also strongly recommended that your committee use and retain a copy of a scoring matrix for each firm you interview. The scoring matrix will help the committee decide on the architect and the direction of the project. Keeping this type of documentation is critical to the long-term success of the project. If decisions are made jointly by a committee, no one will be able to assign individual blame or second-guess the choice of the designer if and when problems or issues arise. This should help keep the focus of discussion on the real issues instead of on assigning

FIGURE 12.2
BUILDING PROFESSIONALS CHART

NEEDS–ASSESSMENT PHASE OF THE PROCESS

KEY PLAYER	RESPONSIBILITY	REPORTS TO	OVERSEES
Taxpayers	Pay for any building improvements		
Library Governing Board	Facilitates the building improvement process	Taxpayers, local government officials	Creating a building advisory committee
Building Advisory Committee consists of library director, representatives from library staff, library governing board, Friends group, community members, and local government officials	Assesses the needs of the community, translates those needs into an RFP, hires an architectural firm, finds the money for the project, provides publicity and support for the project	Taxpayers, library governing board, local government officials	Securing support for the building improvement process
Architectural Firm	Responds to the RFP: meets with the building advisory committee to listen to the goals, dreams, aspirations, and limitations of the library	Building advisory committee	
Building Advisory Committee	Reviews the cost proposal submitted by the chosen architectural firm	Taxpayers, library governing board, local government officials	Engage in the quality-based selection process, whereby the architectural plan is compared to the committee's expectations with a special focus on the cost

78

DESIGN PHASE OF THE PROCESS

Architectural Firm	Design process: Conceptual Schematic 50% 75% 90% Final construction documents	Building advisory committee, which reviews all phases of the process and provides timely feedback, concerns, and approvals so the architect can proceed to the next phase of the process	Completing the phases of the design process

ARCHITECTURAL FIRM'S STABLE OF EXPERTS

Licensed Engineer	Site plan of the design to guarantee that your ground can accommodate the building process	Architectural firm, local building and zoning officials, your neighbors	That your building project does not impact existing structures
Hazardous Remediation Surveyor	Destructive testing to determine if any known hazardous materials will be impacted by your building improvement process	Building advisory committee, architectural firm	The consideration and removal of any toxic materials
Structural Engineer	Determines how your building will be supported	Architectural firm	Designing the bones of the building

(cont.)

FIGURE 12.2 (cont.)

ARCHITECTURAL FIRM'S STABLE OF EXPERTS

KEY PLAYER	RESPONSIBILITY	REPORTS TO	OVERSEES
Mechanical Engineer	Determines how and where your plumbing, heating, cooling, and air-quality equipment will be located	Commissioning agent, who is hired to verify that the initial mechanical design and the final installation meet the design intent	Making sure that the air is fresh, the building is heated and cooled adequately, and the water is delivered and the sewage removed
Electrical Engineer	Interprets National Electric Code and places panels, transformers, and circuits in correct locations/quantities	Architectural firm	Lights and outlets work and don't present a fire hazard
Fire Protection Engineer	Determines where boxes, annunciator panels, and sprinkler systems are to be located	Local fire chief	If there is a fire in the building, notification and management of catastrophe
Lighting Designer	Takes into consideration the uses of the area and proposes the type of lighting systems that can be used for maximum efficacy	Architectural firm	Appropriate lights for each type of use/task
Acoustic Designer	Deals with noise suppression requirements	Architectural firm	Making sure that sound stays where it is supposed to be

Role	Description	Oversight	Responsibility
Data Designer	Looks at the data needs of the facility and adds appropriate wiring to accommodate all computers and other electronic equipment	Building advisory committee, architectural firm	Computer lines and system equipment is adequate for the needs of the building occupants
Security Consultant	Plans for safety and emergency needs of the facility	Building advisory committee, architectural firm	Keeping everyone safe
Interior Designer	Presents a "color board" for approval of interior finishes such as flooring, wall treatments, furnishings	Architectural firm, building advisory committee, library governing board	How the building looks and functions within the structure

POSTDESIGN PHASE OF THE PROCESS: BUILDING IT

Role	Description	Oversight	Responsibility
Clerk of Works	Serves as the advocate, advisor, and watchdog for the building owner	Building advisory committee	The entire process
Job Captain	Oversees the subconsultants once the design is settled	Architectural firm	The successful implementation of the design plan through the employment of skilled personnel

CONSULTANTS AND SUBCONTRACTORS

Role	Description	Oversight	Responsibility
Competent Person	Provides a safe work setting while digging the foundation	Job captain (OSHA mandated)	That the site is safe
Dig Safe Compliance Officer	Locates and marks all existing underground services	Job captain	Maintenance of all existing services that run the property

(cont.)

FIGURE 12.2 (cont.)

KEY PLAYER	RESPONSIBILITY	REPORTS TO	OVERSEES
CONSULTANTS AND SUBCONTRACTORS			
Mason	Builds the foundation	Structural engineer, job captain, clerk of works	Whatever method of foundation is decided upon, this person is responsible for doing the work
Steel Detailer	Draws up plans for needed steel based on the structural engineer's design	Structural engineer, job captain, clerk of works	Defines what steel shapes to buy, what lengths to cut and weld, and where to put the holes for bolting
Roofers	Build the roof members to support the needs of the roof and equipment to be placed on the roof	Structural and mechanical engineers, job captain, clerk of works	Guarantees that the hardest working component of the building is structurally sound and keeps the elements out of the building
Independent Inspector— Roofing	Observes the work being done on your roof and is able to identify problems and quickly make decisions to resolve any issues	Job captain, clerk of works	That your roofing job is done to specifications and all issues are resolved
Window Professionals	Provide a connection between the inside of your building and the outside world	Job captain, clerk of works	Aesthetically pleasing and energy-efficient openings to the neighborhood
Drywallers	Add the interior wall in preparation for finish work	Job captain, clerk of works	A wall . . .

Tapers	Cover the seams of the drywall with successive coats of mud	Job captain, clerk of works	that is solid . . .
Sanders	Smooth out the roughness of the mud and prepare the surface for the finish work (i.e., paint, wallpaper, or cabinetry)	Job captain, clerk of works	and smooth . . .
Painters	Apply a primer and coats of paint to achieve the desired finish	Job captain, clerk of works	and covered with product
Wallpaperers	Apply the sizing and product of choice	Job captain, clerk of works	and covered with product
Millwork Carpenter	Takes the design and translates it into pieces of wood to be assembled on-site	Job captain, clerk of works	and covered with product
Flooring Expert	Installs the flooring finishes	Job captain, clerk of works	Cement, wood, terrazo, or carpet
Ceiling Expert	Installs the ceiling finishes	Job captain, clerk of works	Painted or tiled, a quality job that is safe

personal blame or credit, because personality and personal chemistry will have been minimized as factors in the choices made.

Be aware that during this stage of the process you will be dealing with the architect, but once the plans are drawn up and the work is started the architect will turn your project over to a job captain. There is nothing wrong with this, unless you chose the architect because he promised a level of involvement that isn't being delivered by hiring a job captain. If the architect is up-front with you and tells you that the main contact for your project will be a job captain, then ask to meet that person before your committee makes any decisions. If your committee expected the architect to be the job captain, then you obviously have to rethink the project with that particular firm.

Once your committee makes a decision on the architect they want to design the project, the firm will send you a cost proposal. It is the responsibility of your committee to review the cost proposal for completeness and fairness. The best guide to a fair price is either the percentage of the budget or the cost on a square-foot basis. The firms know how their prices are judged. Some firms proudly promote that they are on the expensive end (ego/status); it is part of their sales package. Your committee will decide if that is an important consideration when making the final decision. Once the cost has been determined, the committee will negotiate the contract to final form with the architectural firm.

This step in the building process is called "quality-based selection." Your committee will take under consideration what the complete package of all the expertise required to get the job done will cost. This is where you compare the committee's expectations with the architectural firm's price. You can expect that the firm knows what it needs to do to give you what you need. It's not inexpensive. It will take a lot of time. As far as you are concerned, when you sign the contract with the architectural firm, the price you agree to pay for the project is what you can expect to pay unless you change the plan in some way. If you don't like the price, say no thanks and call the next firm on your list. Negotiations are over. The next firm will be happy to hear from you. Don't give them a lot of detail on why they were chosen, but give them a feel for your expectations. When negotiating the contract, remember:

1. If the contractor messes up, they may need to do more work, but that won't be your nickel. If they mess up, they put the time in to resolve it for no additional fee. Be tough when it gets to this point.

2. They owe you attendance at the regular job meetings, so you can expect them to know what is going on.

3. They don't do daily quality-control inspections; you need to hire someone to do that. They will only check for "general conformity to the design."

Don't forget that part of the decision process is accepting the architect's stable of subconsultants. You probably won't know them, but it's good to see their credentials and experience. You won't know how much you are paying for them. That is between the designer and the subconsultants.

Once everyone is on board, you need to understand the time frame the architect needs to get the design together. Give them everything they will need to get the planning started. There will be a number of phases in the design process, including conceptual, schematic, 50 percent, 75 percent, and 90 percent phases and the final construction documents. You should expect to receive plans, drawings, and reports from the architectural firm during all these phases. In return, the architect will expect to receive feedback, concerns, and approvals to proceed to the next phase. This process exists so everyone involved in the process can see how the design is developing. You don't want to be faced with a fully detailed design that doesn't work and has not been vetted by those who will use it. Insist on this process for all projects, large or small. Give the review your attention as soon as you can and the degree of attention it deserves. Get the concept, agree on it, see the details, comment on them all, get it drawn up, agree that it is right, and then let it be finished.

INTERIOR DESIGNER

One of the hardest areas to relinquish control of is the interior design. Many of us think we know what we are doing in this area, but the reality is that we should leave the decisions related to our interior to the experts. In libraries you have lots of opportunities to shine or not. Large rooms, high ceilings, and acoustical and lighting considerations require a lot of decisions, and when all of these elements come together they can be a shining example of either good or bad design. Often the interior designer is on the staff of the architect, or is a designer that the architect has worked with successfully before. If you have hired a smaller architectural firm, then sometimes the architect will do the interior design. Remember, the most visible culmination of all the effort that went into the total building process is the interior and how it works to achieve the objectives of the building plan.

The interior design of your building is the showpiece; a building can be stunning on the outside, but poorly conceived interior planning can quickly undermine the total project. The key to getting it right is to make the decisions on the colors and finishes all at the same time. The designer supplies a "color board" for your approval. The discussions you have with the interior designer are as important as the discussions you have had with the architect. Give her the time and consideration that she deserves. Don't rush the process. If you aren't sure how something will look, ask for more clarification or other options. Although you are paying for this expertise, you are also the one who is going to have to live with those hot pink and chocolate walls for the next twenty-five years or more. If you can't see how your plan is going to look, then don't sign off on it; get someone else to look at the plan or propose new ideas. Don't be afraid to trust the designer too. What may seem a little outlandish may fit really well when it all comes together. There is always a current style trend you may not be aware of. Your designer may know these better than you and may be trying to achieve a new, modern style.

If you aren't using an architect, but have a good contractor on a renovation, you may have to work with them to put together the color board. Get three samples of the flooring, a few color chips for the walls, swatches for the wallpaper, and pieces of the finished wood, if you're lucky enough to have this, and put the combinations together and decide what looks right. You should feel very comfortable about the choice when it is done this way. The contractor will be happy about it too. The last thing they need is someone to walk in and question who picked the materials they are working with.

Whether you have had an expert interior designer or have made the interior design decisions with your contractor, if you are walking through the site and something doesn't look right, stop the work. Go back and check your plan. Ask the questions critical to the outcome: "Is that really the right color?" "I thought we were using wallpaper, not paneling," "Isn't that area supposed to be carpeted?" or "Isn't that fireplace supposed to be done in white brick, not orange mosaics?" Don't be afraid to stand up for your project. Mistakes are not uncommon. The paints are ordered by number, and the person doing the work really doesn't know what color you want, so instead of punching in 436, the dyslexic paint attendant punched in 634. One can't be too careful.

HAZARDOUS REMEDIATION SURVEYOR

As much as we would all like to avoid the costs and the work necessary to remediate the hazardous materials in your building, not taking care of these properly can be the most expensive mistake you can make. *With any building over twenty years old, and even some newer ones, you need to be on the lookout for regulated hazardous materials. These can be lead-based paint; PCBs in the lights; mercury in the thermostats, the wiring, or lightbulbs; or asbestos on pipe insulation, piping, siding, mastic, grouts, tile, roofing, and other areas.* Hire a consultant to investigate your building. Give them permission to do destructive testing, and they will generate a report of where your hazardous materials are. Then meet with your architect and get a feel for how much of the hazardous materials will be affected by the renovation. The architect will put together a scope of work that you can use to bid the work out.

If you have hazardous materials in your building, then count on a lot of paperwork, permitting, and clearance testing to get the work done. You don't want to manage this yourself. Your architect and his consultants will most likely refuse to allow this work to be put into their contract. They are not trained or insured to manage this for you. Hire an expert based on the type of hazardous materials you are dealing with.

PROFESSIONAL QUALIFICATIONS

How do you know the architects and other designers are qualified? When you see the name and title of your designers, you may see the letters AIA, or RA, or PE after the name of the individual. If you see Esq., be careful; you are in the wrong room. You'd better not need a lawyer at this point, unless he is just reading the contract before you sign.

- AIA stands for American Institute of Architects. It is the national professional association of architects. The requirements for membership are that the individual is educated and practicing in the field. With that membership the architect has access to information on trends, continuing education, and peer connections to the architectural community.
- RA stands for "registered architect." This is the tough one. It means the individual passed the three-day test.
- PE stands for "professional engineer." These are state-issued registrations. Each state has different requirements for registration, but all encompass qualifying for a series of exams, having the appropriate degree and years of service, being recommended by peers, and having passed the exam. The PE registration is a similar process for all the branches of the engineering community.
- Some states issue licenses denoting the type of professional engineer, be it structural, mechanical, electrical, or fire protection, but many only issue one type of license or stamp.

When one of these professionals passes her respective certifying exam, she gets to buy a stamp with which to emboss original documents. It has her name and a number on it. To earn her pay, she needs to stamp the design documents and place her signature over the stamp. This is not only a professional assurance but carries personal liability as well. There is a code of ethics associated with the stamp that dictates that the professional will only design and stamp work she is qualified to design. The individual is the judge of this. The system works fairly well. The local building inspector who actually gives you the final approval to occupy the building or new renovation is assured that the building is safe and up to code because of the presence of this professional stamp on the drawings.

The codes used in the design are referenced in the building code your jurisdiction uses. Design codes are published by the groups that support the industry. These are not the actual building codes your town and state use but are the referenced processes and details to be done in the code itself. There are codes for masonry, steel, concrete, and wood. When you have a professionally registered engineer on board, it is her duty to meet the prescriptions of these codes. These codes are published by the American Institute of Steel Construction, as well as the Masonry Institute. Proof of compliance for materials is prescribed by the American Society for Testing Materials. Product manufacturers publish data that indicate whether their product meets the standards of the codes. When the designer and contractor follow these codes, it makes for efficient design and construction. (See figure 12.3.)

STRUCTURAL ENGINEER

The structural engineer will decide how your building is going to stand up. She gets the information from the architect on where to place columns and beams and how much space she has to work with. Using math and physics equations, the structural engineer decides on the size of the structures that support the building. There are a lot of software and charts from the building material industry to give her the information she needs to make the right choices. This lets the engineer decide if she wants to use one really thick beam or column, or maybe a few that are smaller.

MECHANICAL ENGINEER

The codes and standards guide decisions on what is needed in the building environment. The codes dictate the required insulation value of the walls and ceilings, the amount of glazing, the amount of fresh air each room in the building will get, and a lot more. There is the state code, and this carries with it the mechanical and plumbing codes and the various fuel codes: one for gas, one for propane, and a different code for fuel oil.

The plumbing codes deal with the safety issues involved with sanitary piping. The waste pipes need to be a certain diameter, and there needs to be venting so the water can flow properly and the sewer gases don't get into the building. When it comes to heating, you want the warm and cold water to get to your sink or heater quickly. This requires pipes and pumps of the right size in the right location so the water moves as it should be moved.

Air needs to move through the building as well. There are codes on how much air movement you need in each room. To provide this, the air ducts need to be located and sized. This is coordinated with the code for air-handling equipment, its size, location, and how it is powered.

It is the mechanical engineer who is responsible for the interpretation of these codes. The mechanical engineer should get the design after the structural designer has made her first pass. This gives the mechanical engineer

---

FIGURE 12.3

SAMPLE BUILDING CODE COMPLIANCE SHEET

Building Code: Occupant Load

Applicable Codes
2006 International Building Code
2006 International Plumbing Code
2008 National Electric Code
2003 NFPA Life Safety Code

Allowable Areas
Actual area 14,323 sq. ft.

Total Occupant Load

Occupant Load	178 people
Egress Capacity	100-inch stair width = 333 people

Library Occupant Load

Total Occupant Load	318 people
Egress Capacity	(2) doors = 92-inch width = 420 people

Occupant Load Used

Classrooms	20 sq. ft./person
Labs	50 sq. ft./person
Offices	100 sq. ft./person
Library Stacks	150 sq. ft./person
Library Reading Rooms	50 sq. ft./person

the information on how much space there is to work with and what type of structure there is to support the piping and ducts. He will draw up the plan showing the ductwork and its size, and there will be a plan with the water pipes, the sewer pipes, and the vent pipes. These plans will show the size and the materials to be used as well.

COMMISSIONING AGENT

A fairly new member of the team is the commissioning agent. This individual is hired to check the mechanical designs and final installation for how well they meet the design intent. One would think that this is the responsibility of the original designer, but the designer isn't tasked with doing a detailed check of the final installation. The commissioning agent exercises some independent oversight of the mechanical designs and final installation. He can help further down the road as well. If you want to know if your system is actually working, and want to take the route of a more "professional" study than you can get from a contractor, the commissioning agent can do it.

FIRE PROTECTION ENGINEER

The code requirements for fire protection will involve an electrical engineer as well as a fire protection engineer. Electrical engineers have to consider the location of the red alarm boxes throughout your building. These need to be located per code and be loud and visible. Your local AHD (authority having jurisdiction), or fire chief, usually has the authority to interpret the design and to add his own requirements. No matter what minimums your designer or the code say, the AHD has the authority to go beyond them, and what he says is final.

If you have a sprinkler system, or have been directed to get one, you may turn to a fire protection engineer. This designer will determine where the sprinkler heads should be located, what size the pipes need to be to feed the sprinkler heads, and how to move the water through the pipes. If you know you need a sprinkler system, you can call a few sprinkler contractors and ask for a design proposal. The work has to be drawn out and stamped before being accepted by the fire chief or the AHD.

Be sure to understand what the designer has in mind for where the pipes go. If you have hard ceilings (i.e., something other than acoustic tile), it will be expensive to hide the pipes. Let your designer know what you want before he starts drawing up the plans. If you need the pipes hidden, you probably want a general contractor involved to take care of the cutting, patching, and painting to hide the pipes.

The sprinkler designer will be responsible for getting approval of the plans from the fire department. This step, although pretty routine, is critical. A big part of the approval process is deciding where the annunciator panels go, as well as how the fire department will respond to a call from your building. The annunciator panels contain the circuiting for the fire alarm control systems. They should include a graphic of the building and possibly a microphone that the fire department can use to broadcast messages within the building.

A big consideration when putting in a sprinkler system is your water supply. If you are on city water, you can have a sprinkler system for far less money than if you are on a well. If you are on well water, you will need to install a large storage tank as well as a powerful pump somewhere on-site to accommodate your sprinkler needs. If you have an AHD ordering you to put these elements in, be sure to make the argument that special financing is needed for you to be able to afford them.

ELECTRICAL DESIGNER

The electricity in your building has to be where you need it, and it must be safe and come in the correct quantity. The licensed electrical contractor is ultimately responsible for this being done properly, but it is the electrical designer who draws up the plan. When you do a renovation or an addition, the power needs of your building change. There are transformers, distribution panels, and circuit systems to be decided on. The electrical designer will locate and size these. The wire size between these points may be shown but more likely will be sized by the contractor. The code used is most likely the National Electric Code.

LIGHTING DESIGNER

Your electrical designer may feel you have greater lighting needs than he is comfortable designing, and so he will engage a lighting designer to assist with the process. This is especially true if you have a room with special or varied needs. If you have an auditorium or large public space, you should have a specialist involved. If you have a main reading room and have a special vision for it, be sure to ask a specialist about how to light it.

This lighting specialist will take into consideration a variety of factors when designing your lighting plan.[2] She will consider the lighting intensity (which is measured in foot-candles), the color of the projected light, and how the light itself works within the greater design. Lighting controls can be pretty intricate. You may decide to have lights with automatic controls, lights controlled by a timer, or a simple switch. The most valuable tool you will see for lighting design is the photometric layout. This is like a topographical map of the light levels. It shows the light intensity at given heights away from the fixture. This helps you determine how many lights you need. You just need to know how bright you want things.

A really nice feature of the available lights is indirect lighting. This is where the light reflects up, off the ceiling. This light is diffused and much softer than direct lighting. Another nice feature is multilevel lighting. This is where there are multiple (three or more) bulbs in the fixture. Depending on how the room is being used at the time, you can set the levels for reading or presenting.

If you have outside lighting to do, you will have to consider how to limit light pollution. Many towns limit how much light can be directed off a site. Lights that meet these criteria have attachments that block the sides and top as required.

ACOUSTIC DESIGNER

Be sure your designer knows the noise suppression requirements necessary in your renovation and how to achieve them. You may even decide to do an acoustic project as a stand-alone project. Specially designed products have sound transmission coefficients associated with them. The equipment in or near the room may need to be dealt with as well. Special construction may be needed to eliminate objectionable noise. You may want special consideration given to your windows if you are in a noisy area.

DATA DESIGNER

Yes, we are in an age with new designers coming on board. Unless you have a good information technology (IT) person, you may want to consider having an independent consultant advise you on necessary IT upgrades. When you choose a data designer, focus on the equipment you have and the number of users you intend to have. That should dictate your needs. There is the consideration of fiber versus copper (go with fiber) and the type of cable (CAT 6E is the standard today, though next week it may be different). You will want to know when wireless is the right choice. (It isn't if you intend to have a lot of users simultaneously with large data input needs.) Ask lots of questions. This technology is changing every day. You don't want last year's technology, but you don't want to build for next year's either, because it will probably be different.

SECURITY CONSULTANT

Before you go out and hire the ex-marine and CIA retiree to advise you on your security needs, decide for yourself what your needs are. You may have a safety committee established within your staff. This group is tasked with identifying and enforcing employee safety and security needs. (The labor laws actually dictate that you have this group in place in your building.) Set up an agenda of security topics and have a brainstorming session. You may find out that you want doors with locks, video cameras, door and window sensors, a protocol for responsibility, procedures for emergencies, and the consideration of exterior lighting. The most important thing really is the training. If everyone feels the issues have been thought through and the important rules and protocols have been identified and assigned, you should have what you need. Then call vendors who sell the stuff and get some pricing. They will give you lots of advice in the process. Once you have the full plan in place, pass it by the AHD and the police department to see if it works for them.

UNIONS

We haven't mentioned unions in this discussion at all. As project facilitator you really shouldn't have to deal with any union-related issues. The role of the construction unions is to delineate which trade does what work and to ensure fair wages and benefits for the trade's people. Trade delineation should be pretty much as you would expect it to be. A couple of quirks might occur when you need a member of the plumbing union to do the water and waste pipes, but the steamfitters' union would do the heating pipes. The caulkers may be part of the carpenters' trade or the masons. Equipment operators get paid differently if they are digging a trench to supply utilities to a building or as part of a highway project.

Unions will sometimes decide that a contractor on the site is not providing proper conditions for the workers, so they may stage a job action. This usually occurs with nonunion or nonsignatory contractors on the site. This is relatively common, even in the more unionized urban areas. This action can legally be limited to picketing the job site. Contractors involved in this should know the drill. If one of your contractors is forced off your job site, you can expect the cost of the job to change, because replacement contractors rarely cost less money. Although this may disrupt the daily flow of your project, you can leave dealing with this up to your contractor. Hold fast on the cost increase, though. He chose the subcontractors, you didn't. Remember too that the public relations work both ways. It's public money you are spending. Those who squeeze pennies get respect too.

AFTER THE DESIGN

Once the plan is decided upon and all the relevant parties have signed off on it, the architect goes to work on coordinating the project. The architect has to make sure the structural designer, in the sizing of the beams, doesn't take the space the mechanical designer needs for his ducts. He needs to be sure all the equipment the mechanical designer put in is picked up on the electrical plan. He needs to make sure that all of the items requiring plumbing on the initial plan were caught by the mechanical engineer.

One of the major reasons for claims by contractors is when this coordination is wrong. The architect's plan may show a sink in the library that the plumber missed. The contractor will want to get paid extra for this. You will ask why, because the sink was on the plan. The answer is that the plumber didn't bid the architect's plan. The resolution can go either way. If you refuse to pay the extra charge, the contractor will have to work it out with the plumber or tell the designer he has to pay for it. This lack of coordination, while it bogs down the process, shouldn't derail the plan. It is a classic case of not sweating the small stuff and deciding which battles are really worth fighting. This can be a tough call.

Once the job gets under way, the subconsultants are the first line in quality control. The contractor is required to submit "shop drawings" of all the materials they will be supplying. With a fully designed plan, the requirements are fully detailed. On the smaller work, write it into the contract. The subconsultants approve it, you get a copy, and now you know what to look for on the job. At the end of the job you get a book of operation and maintenance manuals that reiterate all that was provided. This requirement covers all the trades. It will include not just equipment cuts but design plans as well. Examples of this are the foundation reinforcing, or the structural steel, full-scale drawings for millwork, sprinkler systems, and other considerations. This process is where the design is finally completed.

NOTES
1. American Institute of Architects, www.aia.org/index.htm.
2. Libris Design, "Lighting for Libraries," http://librisdesign.org/docs/ LightingLibraries.pdf.

13 | CONTRACTS AND LEGAL OBLIGATIONS

YOU'VE DECIDED TO go ahead with your project, you have a firm picked out, and you know what you have in the budget, so let's get it in writing. Big or small, whenever you are doing a building project that involves multiple players, you need a contract. What will this look like, who writes it, and what should be in it? Who better to write the contract than you, the one most familiar with the project? You know what you want done, you know when it needs to be done, and you know what kinds of interruptions, noise levels, and dust levels your daily operations can tolerate within work hours. Start the process of writing the contract by making a list of the tasks your designer or contractor has told you he is going to do.

Your contract should include all the plans that already exist, as well as any specification sheets that have been developed. Include in the contract information about the payment process, how to address problems with the contractor or designer, and any other issues you have discussed with your design committee. Consider the contract to be a document that enables you and your contractor to keep clear who is doing what, when, where, and how.

Put in as much detail as you can. Writing a good contract with lots of detail will give all parties involved a mechanism by which to remain focused, resolve issues, and avoid headaches down the road. Those you are contracting with will of course have their own templates and will provide these to you as the contract. These are a good resource and will have a lot of the information you will want in the final document. Feel free to cross out and add whatever you like. If the other party balks, remember that you can say good-bye. You may be in a rush to get going and may fear losing time, but not having the right contract can result in a project experience you will hate.

With the designer, the key to a good contract is to list what you agree they are not going to do. This needs to be a short list. The things you wrongly assume they will be doing will be expensive to add in later. If they say no to some items you want them to do, be sure you understand how you will get those services done. Adding components to your project after the design has been finalized is very expensive. Make sure everything you need to have included in the plan is done before you sign any contracts. Not only will you save lots of money and have fewer sleepless nights, but the time you save will be huge as well.

The design component of the contract will include several pages delineating who's who, what's going to be done, the payment schedule broken down by percentages as well as target payment dates, who covers what, and the insurance requirements for the project. If you are providing information (i.e., plans or other studies) to the designer, this needs to be part of the contract too. You can list them as a reference, but you need a complete copy of the documents with the original contract.

For the contract with the contractor, the package will be big. It will include not only who does what but also the details of managing the work, your rights to access, power, utilities, supervision, and the technical specifications for the project. Everything to be provided and installed is described in full detail in the contract. These are the plans. A minimum of three complete packages need to be created: one for you, one for your job supervisor, and one for the contractor. Each package needs to be complete. It should have the plans and specs and the contract with the owner and contractor, including the insurance contractor, and all the legal paperwork the financial and legal departments require for the contract to be executed. The contract language specifies what you own, what you are paying for, and what the contractor must give you. It's often said the best contract is the one you never have to read, and that is true. But remember, it's not true that if the document doesn't exist, then you have negligence.

A template will help you organize your information and guarantee that everything that needs to be included in the contract is taken into consideration. Professional organizations produce contract templates for their respective trades. Architectural designers contact the AIA, and contractors contact the Association of General Contractors, the union-based representative organization for contractors. The open shop (nonunion)–based organization is the Association of Builders and Contractors. It really is best to write down what you know you need and want, then go to the templates. Included there is a list of items you want to see in a contract. You may be surprised to see this much detail, but imagine your surprise if you don't include everything that needs to be in the contract.

DAVIS-BACON ACT

If your project involves federal funding or has the stipulation that your contractor must pay prevailing wages, you may face union wage scales and job descriptions. These standards and regulations are meant to ensure that the trades get paid a fair, balanced wage. It also protects owners from unscrupulous contractors who win projects by paying low wage rates. Municipalities often turn to the established union rates to set the prevailing wages. The legislation is called the Davis-Bacon Act. It is not a mandate to use union labor but is sometimes misinterpreted as a requirement to do so. It does give the union a better chance of winning work because the unions often provide benefits, and the act requires including the cost of benefits in the equation. This legislation is common for federal and some state work. Locally funded work would depend on your municipality. Even with this, it is not a difficult requirement to meet the wages paid criteria. Remember, good contractors pay their skilled laborers what they are worth; you get what you pay for.

The hardest part of following Davis-Bacon is that someone has to keep track of everyone who has worked on the job and get a verifiable record of their pay. Interviews are done under the federal rules as spot checks to test the system. It is a lot of paperwork. If you have this requirement, you as the receiver of the funds will be tasked with it. Try to have the town hire a firm or individual who is familiar with the law to take care of it. Figure at least ten hours a week in the budget for this work.

INSURANCE

Everybody involved on the job needs insurance, especially the workers. You may already have an insurance carrier that holds a policy on your building. They could be the best source for advice on what you should look for in policies from your designers and contractors. You will want to see coverage for builder's risk. This covers your building while work is being done. You can buy this yourself, or you can have the contractor provide it. The insurance needs to cover your entire building, not just the part they are working on or the value of the work they are performing.

The insurance policy must show liability coverage and automobile coverage. All the workers will have vehicles on your property, so they all need to be insured. Workers' compensation insurance is typically mandated by state law, so you would expect it to be in place, but with any insurance, it's not a bad idea to prove the coverage exists. You may be surprised to find that workers' compensation coverage does not exist for all trades; when you have an owner operator, or sole proprietorship, you may find it is not required by law, so it won't be there. This is sometimes used to get around protecting all the individuals on the site, however. All your workers could be sole proprietorships. This isn't legal. They need to be covered by an employer. Insist on seeing the documentation and reject the assertion that they are "independents." You could insert a line in the general contractor's contract that no workers are to be on the site without workers' compensation. It's good to put language dictating this in the up-front construction documents so the bidders know what you want.

BONDS

You are going to be looking for performance and payment bonds as well. These are basically a financial guarantee that the contractor finishes the job and that everyone who supplies labor or materials is paid. A recognized bonding company will provide a performance bond document stating the contract is bonded to a certain amount. If your contractor fails, you call the bonding company and they are obligated to provide the resources to finish the job. They will have to pay to hire a new contractor to get the job done. In the event of a big problem, the act of formally notifying the bonding company is a very effective tool and often is as far as you need to go to get the resolution you want.

The method used to call in the bonding company needs to be in your contract. This is usually as simple as your putting the contractor on formal, written notice that they are not meeting the contract requirements and that they have a set number of hours to change this situation. After that, you have the right to invoke the bond. A phone call to the bonding company before you mail the notice can be very helpful, but don't be afraid to send it. You will be past any bluffing stage if you are talking to the bonding company. It is in the bonding company's best interest to convince the contractor to make you happy.

The payment bond is invoked if your general contactor goes out without paying all the subcontractors and material providers. If you get a notice from a subcontractor that they are owed money, you forward this to your bonding company. Most laws require the receiver of goods to pay the provider. If you don't have proof the provider has been paid, you have to pay them. A lien release provides you with protection from this, without the need to invoke the bond.

Lien releases exist to protect suppliers from unscrupulous contractors. Some contractors order material or services from a subcontractor or material supplier, install it on the job, bill the owner, and get paid for it, and then never pay the material supplier. Liens are legal notifications that the supplier provided a product and has rights to the property until they get paid. These rules exist to allow contractors to put a lien on a property as soon as they begin work on a project. Hopefully, the law in your area requires them to tell you, the owner, that they have this right and will use it if necessary. This is helpful to you because now you know who has to get paid.

The law allows subcontractors and material providers to take action against you if they haven't been paid, even if you paid the general contractor. The lien release provides limited protection to you against having to pay twice. The lien release protects the rights of the material supplier for a specified portion of the work. You can require the contractor to have every subcontractor who is included on prior payment requests to confirm they got their money and release the right to call for it. This limits your liability to one monthly payment. This should be an absolute requirement for all commitments of $5,000 or more. (You can't require all; some may involve small amounts from, say, the local hardware store.) At the end of the job you get a final release from the contractor. This needs to be signed by an authorized corporate entity and notarized.

PAYMENT APPLICATIONS

Deciding how much to pay the contractor or designer as work progresses is a very straightforward process. It has to be. It is an affirmation of trust and a de facto acknowledgment of your acceptance of the work. To be that it needs to happen promptly. To make that happen, we ask the contractor to provide a "schedule of values" for the work. This is a breakdown of all the parts of the contract, adding up to the total contract value. The breakdown is by trade. There is a section on management, called "general conditions," then one on all the trades that will be working at your site—painters, carpentry, roofing contractors, mechanical, and so on. You need to accept a list of values for the different parts of the work, and this is what the contractor will bill against. When reviewing the list, you'll need to watch out for front-end loading, which is when the contractor places a high value on portions of the work that are done early and a lower value on work done toward the end. This makes the value for site work more than it actually cost, while things like painting are valued at less than their actual cost. In this way, the contractor gets the money before he has earned it. Each month, or whatever period you agree to, the contractor sends an invoice with money allotted to the parts of the master list that have been done. It's easy to review and accept this invoice, or to ask for revisions.

Most contracts include provisions for retaining. This is a percentage of the total payment for the project that you hold back for final acceptance. This is held in case there is a problem with the work you are agreeing to pay for. This varies between 5 and 10 percent. You hold this money until a month or two after the entire project is finished. It also acts as insurance to get the contractor back to finish those irritating little items that pop up at the end of every project. When you have changes and add this value to the contract, these are added to the schedule of values to create a new bottom line. The contractor then bills against this work as it is completed, just as he did with all the other items.

CLERKS

Unless you have an extraordinary amount of faith in your contractor or you have a qualified person in the construction business on your staff, you may feel more comfortable with the work if you have a person assigned to the project who is watching out for your interest. This position is called the clerk of works. This position can often be a double-edged sword. The clerk is in a position where he needs to establish to you that he is capable and that you are getting value for his services. Establishing this may be at the expense of your contractors and designers. It takes a highly qualified professional to provide this value without undermining your contractor. If you or members of your staff or design team can be close enough to the work to have a good sense of the level of quality, you may want to save the expense of having a clerk. Local or state laws regarding spending capital funds may dictate that you have a clerk, or your municipality may have an individual who is regularly asked to perform these functions, so you may have no choice.

With all the levels of responsibility on a construction project, it is important to keep an open mind and listen to all sides of an issue when one is brought to your attention. Reported problems may have been identified by your clerk, or they may be so new that your contractor may have just been made aware of them. The contractor may be ready, willing, and able to effect the resolution; he just needs the opportunity to do it.

CLOSEOUT/PUNCH LIST

You've got a date established for when the work will be done, and you have a plan in place to occupy the space; *now you need the process to effect the turnover.*

The contractor will have your schedule on moving in. This needs to be developed from there. This process involves getting all the trades done and moved out. They then give you a date to do the "punch list." This is when your designer and you or your staff designee inspect the work with a fine-tooth comb. The more thorough you are, the happier the contractor will be. It is the tradespeople who are accountable. All will be thankful that they know what they need to do. This is why it's important to be as thorough as possible. Be prepared to spend half an hour or more per room checking everything out.

If there are mechanical components, there will be balancing reports to be provided by the contractor showing you how the air and water systems are working. Your mechanical design consultant will review these and go through the project to inspect the components. If you have a commissioning agent, he will be on a different schedule; his work is completed after the contractor has left and the building is in use. You and your contractor then agree to a time frame for completion of the punch list and you agree on the time frame for the move.

To be done, paperwork detailed in the contract and specification sheets needs to be submitted, reviewed, and accepted by the designer and yourself. This includes warranties, as-builts, and operation and maintenance manuals.

THE CONTRACTS

So let's take a look at a design contract. The format and goals of the construction and design contracts will be the same. The items you need to see in the design contract are as follows:

1. Title
2. Owner
    a. Description of project
    b. Designer
3. Authority of signatory
4. Description of services
5. Design, research, drafting, etc.
6. Description of the payment process
    a. Hourly rates
    b. Reimbursables
        i.   Mileage
        ii. Copying
        iii. Travel expenses
    c. Payment schedule
7. Design responsibility
    a. Hazardous materials
    b. Subconsultants' responsibility
    c. Exclusions
8. Rights of the owner
    a. Right to add or remove scope
    b. Ownership of product
    c. Right to occupy
9. Design guidelines
10. Construction guidelines
11. Schedule and description of deliverables (basic services)
    a. Schematic phase
    b. Design development phase
    c. Construction documents
    d. Construction bidding
    e. Construction administration
12. Owner responsibility
    a. Designate representative
    b. Duty to inspect, accept, and pay
13. Termination rights
    a. Funding removed
    b. Failure to perform
14. Claims process
    a. Arbitration, mediation, civil action
15. Insurance and indemnification requirements
16. Authorized signatures

A construction contract will consist of the following:

1. Invitation to bid
2. Executed bid documents
3. General conditions
4. Drawings and specifications, including all addenda issued prior to execution of the contract, wage scales where applicable
5. Bonds where required
6. Insurance certificates
7. Other documents listed in the "agreement and modification" issued after the execution of the contract, change orders, and alteration orders issued in accordance with part 12 of the "general conditions" section

So what is the "general conditions" section of the contract? This is the meat of your rights and responsibilities while the job is under way. Design forms will have a basic template of these. Read them carefully and plug in what you need. They will be short on the details specific to your job, so they will need some editing.

The table of contents of the "general conditions" section will include the following:

PART	ITEM	PART	ITEM
1	Definitions	12	Changes in Work
2	Contract Documents	13	Patents
3	Notice	14	Assignments
4	Access to the Work	15	Superintendence by Contractor
5	Accident Protection		
6	Hazardous Materials	16	Failure to Complete Work on Time
7	Subcontracts		
8	Responsibility of Contractor to Act in Emergency	17	Substantial Completion and Final Inspection
		18	Default and Termination of Contract
9	Mutual Responsibility of Contractors	19	Termination of Contract without Fault
10	Payments to Contractor	20	Assignment Provision
11	Contractor's Title to Materials		

Then there are the plans and specification sheets. Most projects are broken into sixteen sections or divisions, most describing a certain trade (i.e., section 3 is concrete, section 6 is carpentry, while owner stuff is sections 0 and 1).

DIVISION 0	**MISCELLANEOUS DOCUMENTS**
001	Table of Contents
002	Project Directory
003	Drawing List
BIDDING	**REQUIREMENTS**
004	Invitation to Bid
005	Instructions to Bidders
006	Information Available to Bidders
007	Proposal Form Lump Sum Grand Total Bid
008	Required Information from the Bidder
DIVISION 1	**GENERAL REQUIREMENTS**
1001	General Conditions
1002	Price and Payment Procedures
1003	Administrative Requirements
1004	Submittal Procedures
1005	Execution Requirements

Then the document gets into the technical specifications:

DIVISION 2	**SITE CONSTRUCTION**
DIVISION 3	**CONCRETE**
DIVISION 4	**MASONRY**
. . . and so on	

CLOSING

The bigger the dollar value of the contract and the more professional involvement you have had in the development of the project, the more levels of legalese and contract requirements you will have. They boil down to these basics:

Who
> Owner
> Contractor

What
> The plans (these are the drawings)
> The specifications (the written descriptions of the work)

Why (is either side doing this)
> Payment
> Project deliverables (the building, the as-built documents)

When
> The schedule

Everything else in the contract consists of definitions and the controls in place to protect these basics. Don't get hung up on these definitions and controls. If you have lawyers involved, encourage them to get the contract agreed to and signed, then stick it in the bottom drawer and watch the job get done. Just keep three things in front of you at all times:

1. The finish dates. Not meeting them or not changing them when you both know you need to will lead to confusion and lots of misunderstandings.

2. The price. It will change with change orders. (When there is a change request, agree or disagree and move forward, quickly. If the contractor doesn't accept your position, they can petition you later.) Keep the cost in front of you the whole time. You can easily overspend if you don't do this.

3. The current plans. Every change has a description. Be sure you and the person in charge of building it have the change written down where it is going to be seen.

That is it. Remember, the good contracts are the ones you never have to read or refer to. Most jobs go like this. Don't forget to enjoy the experience. Even when it's tough, the construction project itself will be as memorable as the finished product.

<table>
<tr><td>14</td><td># NEW TECHNOLOGY AND CONCLUDING REMARKS</td></tr>
</table>

EVERYONE IS TALKING about "going green" these days, and many companies are making a lot of money selling their snake oil as "green" products. Care must be taken to look at the products and equipment that are used in your building in order to spot green initiative impostors. If the product is being shipped 8,000 miles across the ocean, then it isn't green. If the product has lots of ingredients that you can't pronounce, it isn't green. We should all ask three questions about our building:

1. What does my building use that is part of the natural cycle of the earth?

2. What does my building use that can never be replaced?

3. What harm comes from the operation of my building?

If everyone started asking these questions seriously, then every environment would be healthier, more energy efficient, and have less of a long-lasting negative impact on the globe.

You need to be able to understand how to minimize your building's energy impact on your own, on a regular basis. Integrate the three key questions into every purchasing decision you make. Do your research when replacing key energy-expending equipment. This is where the return on investment discussion becomes important. Consult free experts like the U.S. Green Building Council (USGBC; www.usgbc.org) when making decisions. Their website, and similar sites, offer lots of information to help you make decisions. Weigh all the options. Organizations like the USGBC have made considerable headway in identifying and quantifying those aspects of our work environment that affect the global environment. These organizations also reward and recognize projects that minimize the impact of our spaces on the environment. Although achieving these certifications is admirable, it does take a considerable commitment, may be expensive, and may not be possible for the majority of old libraries. You can, however, use these organizations to look for models and do what you can within your own organization. Read the case studies at these sites; there is no sense reinventing the wheel. Remember, even if your building is not USGBC-certified, every small change we make in our world helps the global environment.

Although being green is an admirable goal, a better way to think is in terms of sustainability. Sustainability takes into consideration everything that is used in your building: where the item comes from and whether or not it can be replaced. When looking at your building, the most important item in the sustainability equation is the energy it uses to maintain a comfortable environment. Remember, energy is used for heating, cooling, air-conditioning, humidity control, interior and exterior lighting, and every piece of electronic equipment that is used as system support. Every appliance, heating unit, air-conditioning unit, computer monitor, computer printer, computer tower, boiler, dehumidifier, and light uses energy in the form of electricity or fuel. Our goal should be twofold: (1) to find equipment that takes less energy to operate, and (2) to find alternatives to traditional types of energy so we are not using nonrenewable resources wastefully.

Let's start with the heating and cooling equation. When a new building is constructed, we find that efforts to minimize energy use are now automatically incorporated into the project. A new building or finished product will use fewer resources than the old one did. If you can't build a new state-of-the-art library, then the first step is to identify what is using energy in your building and how much. As we discussed earlier, the efficacy of your building's heating and cooling equipment is determined by your building envelope and the efficiency of the equipment. Before spending lots of money installing an expensive, high-efficiency heating/cooling system, you should plan on improving your building envelope first. If you have a poorly insulated structure, then even the most efficient furnace isn't going to keep you warm and will run just as much as your old furnace. The furnace may cost less to run, but you will still be wasting nonrenewable resources heating the outdoors.

The first step you should take is an analysis to see how well insulated your building is. This is important in a cold environment and even more so in warm climates, because cooling a building actually requires more energy per degree than heating a building. The wall, roof, and foundation insulation need to be complete and well maintained to give you the maximum savings on your heating bill. If your building is more than ten years old, then you should expect that your building envelope is less than efficient. The real push for energy efficiency in building design didn't really gain momentum until the 1980s. Most buildings before then weren't designed with efficiency in mind or built with materials that have a long-term efficacy.

A relatively new type of service is offered by contracted energy auditors. The auditors will assess your building envelope to help you see where energy is being wasted in it. The energy auditor will photograph your building using an infrared camera. This camera takes a picture that shows the heat signature of your building. Your building will look like a multicolored blob, with the color red indicating heat. The red zones are where the heat is escaping. If there is a predominance of red in your picture, then your building is losing heat and therefore wasting both money and nonrenewable resources. Use these pictures to see where you need to make the corrections and ask the auditors to give you advice on low-cost ways to minimize your heat loss.

Once you've taken care of your building envelope, you can start thinking about new heating equipment to minimize your energy use. The energy auditors or even the equipment providers can help you calculate the payback time for new equipment: the return on investment. In most cases you will still be using traditional fossil fuels—just less of them, hopefully. The next question becomes, what equipment can you purchase that uses other types of energy, thus keeping your energy footprint minimal?

HEATING

The boiler plant can be designed to use a variety of fuels. Traditional oil is efficient, but it is a fossil fuel. The boiler plant could use coal, but that too is a fossil fuel. Industry is developing new technology to lessen the amount of carbon released into the atmosphere when coal is burned, but this technology has not been widely adopted yet. Wood is coming into greater use. Wood-chip furnaces on a building-sized scale are in use. The technology is simple but is space- and labor-intensive. You have to refill the firebox and the storage pile on a regular basis. Wood is a good choice in areas where the local economy supports the wood industry. Wood pellets are an established technology. The pellets are a manufactured product from waste wood, but again you must keep the firebox and storage area full. Pellets burn very hot. An auger turns to supply the pellets to the firebox, so be forewarned: if the power fails, there are no pellets fed to the firebox, and therefore no heat.

Even with wood producing a carbon-based exhaust, the benefit here is that it is today's carbon, not that from 300 million years ago. This makes it carbon-neutral. Other fuels are in the works based on new organics. These would include ethanol-based products (which have been shown to have a significant impact on the world food supply), as well as fuels derived from fast-growing materials such as algae. Once you settle on the type of fuel your building will use, then the next step is to look at a delivery system for the desired product of the fuel—energy.

RADIANT HEAT

How you get the heat to where you want it in the building does make a big difference in your building's energy efficiency. One option used in certain installations is radiant floors. Radiant floors are great if you have a concrete floor and don't plan on carpeting your building, because the carpet acts as an insulator. Before using this system, be sure your designer has experience working with radiant concrete floors. The concrete slab isn't like a radiator that can be turned on and off; instead, it is a big heat sink. You want it warm in the fall and cool in the spring. You need an air system or additional baseboards to cover the extremes of winter and summer. Another type of radiant heat has been introduced in panels. These panels aren't the most efficient method, because by design the heat they release is in places we don't want it, high up in the room. They can be placed in areas where you need heat; for example, perhaps your current heating system can't be modified to accommodate a new area of the building; panels could be added to heat this area.

GREEN ROOFS

These fall into the category of envelope improvement because they greatly reduce the heating and cooling load of your building. Green roofs minimize the runoff of rainwater into the environment. They also reduce a building's heat signature. Roofs typically have been black, and this absorbs heat from the sun and warms the surroundings. Green roofs absorb less heat. There are a variety of approaches to the green roof. Some involve designs for an actual garden structure on the roof. The roof will have soil and drainage, as well as the plants. This is a very high-cost option. The design of a green roof must take into consideration the extra weight and drainage needs of the garden space. The other type of green roof design is actually a quite simple and effective method, sort of like bucket gardening with tomatoes. All the plants are in a tray. There is a drainage mat under them so you don't interrupt the original flow characteristics of the roof. Suppliers for this vegetation are widely available. Don't pay too much for these plants. The cost to produce them isn't much different than that of garden-variety plants.

LIGHTING

Lighting is the biggest user of electricity in a building. Installing new lights that use more efficient bulbs can make a big impact on your utility bill. There are a number of new types of lighting technology, such as LED lighting (light-emitting diodes), that can be quickly installed within your building. This new technology emits light that is a different color, with a different diffusing pattern, and often with less heat (thus reducing your cooling bills). Check out a few installations with a lighting expert to see how the different lights look before committing to a project. The last thing you want is light that doesn't fit the needs of your space, even if the new fixtures use less energy.

An additional way to save electricity in lighting is with the use of motion sensors. As the name implies, when motion is sensed, the lights are turned on, and after a set amount of time they turn off. The use of this technology is long overdue. Using a motion sensor is an easy modification to the lighting power circuit. Motion sensor lights can be included on normal switching circuits as well, so if you need to you can bypass the sensor and operate the lights manually.

COOLING

Your cooling needs are met with electrically powered technology. The cool air is produced by pumps that compress a gas and power fans that eject heat from the cooling fluid in your system. To improve your energy footprint you need to use electricity not produced by fossil fuels or use less of it.

GEOTHERMAL

Geothermal technology offers an alternative cooling strategy by supplying a cooling base fluid without the aid of a utility. Instead of cooling the liquid with compressors, you use liquid that is already cooled: water from within the earth. Though you are using earth-cooled liquid, the process to move the fluid requires the use of pumps powered by electricity. Many buildings use these geothermal systems for heating as well, but the equation doesn't work anywhere near as well for this purpose. The earth has an average temperature of about 55° F. That is a good temperature to use for cooling purposes on a 90° day, because you have a 35° difference to work with, but that same 55° is not to going to warm your building when the outside temperature is 50° F or lower. Geothermal uses a lot of energy to produce this 5° difference. There is a significant amount of energy needed to make this system work during colder temperatures, and electricity is an inefficient heat source.

PHOTOVOLTAICS

Photovoltaics, which use solar cells to convert sunlight directly into electricity, are considered the wave of the future. The production of this safe and effective technology has been "doubling every 2 years, increasing by an average of 48 percent each year since 2002."[1] These systems require expensive materials and construction and do take a fair share of maintenance, but the outcome, a clean and efficient energy source, is worth the expense. The cost of this technology has been dropping, and its use is becoming more widespread. When you look into a technology that can make a real difference in your electric bill, you will find that photovoltaics offer a very long payback.

WIND

Local wind is expensive, unpredictable, and maintenance-intensive. The ability to put wind-generated electric power into your building requires switching devices that cost as much as the windmill. The payback on wind power for a commercial building is not balancing out at this time. Utility-scale wind power is making a difference, however. These units are very big and thus are able to offer more consistency in their power generation. The technology is standardized (patented equipment controls the market). If you have the option to buy "green" power, some of your bill should go to supporting these installations.

CONCLUSION

As we move forward with building technology, these more efficient and environmentally friendly choices will become more mainstream, thus more affordable. Keep your mind open to these technologies. Study the evolution of the technology, and when it is time to make a purchasing decision, look at all the options available to you, not just the traditional ones. Remember to ask your vendors and installers for the information you will need to adequately rate the equipment's return on investment. Don't tie yourself to one technology. If it is going to take too long for the equipment in your favored technology to pay for itself, then look at alternatives. Because you are working with public funds, you owe your taxpayers the consideration that their money is being used as efficiently as possible. Whenever you need to replace equipment, look at your long-range planning and include these new technologies as your targets as they become more affordable choices. Who knows, someday soon photovoltaic energy may be the norm, and there will be other cutting-edge technologies on the horizon!

NOTE

1. Robert Kropp, "Solar Expected to Maintain Its Status as the World's Fastest-Growing Energy Technology," Social Funds, www.socialfunds.com/news/article.cgi/2639.html.

RESOURCES

Alter, Lloyd. "12 Ways to Green Your Home for Winter: What Gives You the Most Bang for the Buck Look." Treehugger.com, October 6, 2008. www.treehugger.com/files/2008/10/12-ways-to-green-your-house-for-winter.php. Explore the website for other simple ways to make a difference.

American Institute of Architects. www.aia.org/index.htm.

CellularWindowShades.com. http://cellularwindowshades.com.

Energy Star. Portfolio Manager. www.energystar.gov/index.cfm?c=evaluate_performance.bus_portfoliomanager. This is a great resource that will help you evaluate the performance of your building.

Energy Star. Reflective Roof Products for Consumers. www.energystar.gov/index.cfm?c=roof_prods.pr_roof_products. This site is a great resource that will help you evaluate the performance of your roof, as well as offering suggestions for roofing materials.

FacilitiesNet. "From Audit to Action: Roof Coating Keeps Company Cool." May 13, 2009. This article on the FacilitiesNet website presents a case study of a roof coating that reflects heat and reduces energy costs. Explore the other case studies on the site for more ideas.

Look Up. www.changehappensindegrees.org/lookup-thermostats-fans.aspx. This site discusses the proper use of ceiling fans, programmable thermostats, and other energy-saving ideas.

Malman, David. "Lighting for Libraries." Libris Design Project. 2005. http://librisdesign.org/docs/LightingLibraries.pdf.

McGraw Hill Construction. Continuing Education Center. "What's So Cool about Cool Roofs?" March 2009. This article presents some facts and follow-up studies on various roofing alternatives.

National Fenestration Rating Center. "The Facts about Windows and Heat Loss." January 2005. www.nfrc.org/documents/U-Factor.pdf.

Sands, Johanna. "Sustainable Library Design." Libris Design Project. N.d. http://librisdesign.org/docs/SustainableLibDesign.pdf. Libris Design is the best resource out there for information on how to make your library more energy efficient, with a quest for sustainability.

Siliski, Andrew. "Everyday Environmental Stewardship: Monitoring Utility Use and Cost." Massachusetts Interfaith Power and Light. N.d. This article provides example spreadsheets and outlines the types of data you should be collecting to better understand the energy your building is using.

Tait, Jason. "Library Ahead of Its Time; Uses Energy Deep within the Earth for Heating, Cooling." *Eagle-Tribune.* March 21, 2007. www.eagletribune.com/punewshh/local_story_080093923.

U.S. Department of Energy. Federal Energy Management Program. Operations and Maintenance Best Practices Guide. July 2004. www1.eere.energy.gov/femp/operations_maintenance/om_bpguide.html. This site is an excellent place to turn when you are trying to understand how your equipment works and how to better maintain it for energy-efficient operation.

U.S. Department of Energy. National Renewable Energy Laboratory. "Cooling Your Home Naturally." October 1994. www.nrel.gov/docs/legosti/old/15771.pdf. This is an easy-to-understand, concise review of how to affordably keep your building more comfortable.

The Warm Company. www.warmcompany.com. This company manufactures the materials needed to produce and use window quilts successfully.

INDEX

You may also be interested in

Countdown to a New Library, Second Edition: Writing from the perspective of a librarian who has been through numerous building projects, Jeannette Woodward walks you through the process of overseeing the planning and execution of facility construction and renovation..

Designing Space for Children and Teens in Libraries and Public Places: Providing tips, suggestions, and guidelines on the critical issues that surround designing spaces for children and teens, this how-to book will help you create a space that they will never want to leave.

Moving Your Library: Author and experienced mover Steven Carl Fortriede has everything you need to get the job done quickly and efficiently with step-by-step directions, diagrams, spreadsheets, and photos.

Public Libraries Going Green: This is the first book to focus strictly on the library's role in going green, helping you with collection development, disposal, and recycling issues; green equipment, technology, and facilities; programming ideas; ways to get the community involved in the process; and more.

Order today at www.alastore.ala.org or 866-746-7252!

Library Use Only

CPSIA information can be obtained at www.ICGtesting.com
Printed in the USA
239311LV00002B/54/P